LOW-MAINTENANCE
BONSAI

Low-Maintenance
BONSAI

Herb Gustafson

Sterling Publishing Co., Inc.
New York

Edited and page layouts designed by
Jeanette Green

Library of Congress Cataloging-in-Publication Data Available

1 3 5 7 9 10 8 6 4 2
Published by Sterling Publishing Company, Inc.
387 Park Avenue South, New York, N.Y. 10012
© 1999 by Herb L. Gustafson
Distributed in Canada by Sterling Publishing
℅ Canadian Manda Group, One Atlantic Avenue, Suite 105
Toronto, Ontario, Canada M6K 3E7
Distributed in Great Britain and Europe by Cassell PLC
Wellington House, 125 Strand, London WC2R 0BB, England
Distributed in Australia by Capricorn Link (Australia) Pty Ltd.
P. O. Box 6651 Baulkham Hills, Business Centre, NSW 2153, Australia
Printed in Hong Kong

Sterling ISBN 0–8069–6211–9

CONTENTS

PREFACE

On first inspection, the term *low-maintenance bonsai* seems like an oxymoron. Bonsai, as plants, generally require more patience, attention, and horticultural experience than any of the other garden-related hobbies. In most cases, however, lack of success is mistaken for a high degree of difficulty. In all aspects of growing bonsai, we have decisions to make: what size of pot, type of plant, soil mixture, and more. In all cases, we have the opportunity to make our job easier and, therefore, increase our chances of not only keeping our bonsai alive, but vigorous as well.

In each chapter of this book, we will explore the ways we can make our daunting task a bit easier—even fun! Every aspect of successful bonsai growing has its shortcuts, new ideas, and time-saving techniques favored by experienced professionals and amateurs alike. Indeed, I have used many of these tricks for nearly forty years without really thinking about them until I became aware of the problems faced by students. This book may fill a surprising gap in existing bonsai literature: how to ensure success by eliminating the common shortfalls that beginners inadvertently get themselves into. You'll find the correct pot, use the best soil, and improve on a dozen other facets of bonsai horticulture simultaneously. Your task will turn magically into a pastime of joy, personal confidence, and inner peace. Bonsai was never meant to be a formidable hurdle with intimidating rules and regulations.

Watching your trees grow and develop year after year can give you one of your greatest pleasures. Remember: the only "finished" bonsai is a dead one. We grow with our trees. We need to recognize that their annual rings are also ours. Enjoy this time together.

—Herb Gustafson

I would like to thank Joyce Temby for her organization and word processing and for the filing necessary for preparation of the book manuscript. I very much appreciate her continued support and encouragement.

I received valuable input on plant selection for chapter two, which considers plants suitable for bonsai, from the Internet Bonsai Club. Thanks to you from all parts of the globe, especially Reiner Goebel, Nina Shishkoff, Walter Pall, Luis Fontanills, Brent Walston, Mary Miller, Ernie Kuo, Alan Walker, and Jim Lewis.

Thanks to Bob Baltzer for allowing me to take fall photographs of Japanese maple foliage at his nursery.

And thanks to Annie Dog—pest, shadow, pleasant distraction, and faithful companion at my feet while I write.

CHAPTER ONE

POTS

1-1. Choose from these eleven pots one that will suit your bonsai.

CHOOSING A POT

Many sizes, shapes, and colors of containers are made for bonsai. They come from several countries and are made of a variety of materials. In this chapter, we will explore how we can create low-maintenance bonsai by choosing our pots carefully. Let's consider a few of the various types of containers available to us. From front to back and from left to right in photo **1–1** (above), let's look at each pot to get an idea of how to begin selecting an appropriate container for our tree.

First, there's an earth-brown unglazed container of Japanese origin. Its gently curved sides and long legs complement a slender, curving trunk. The unglazed brown color looks best with an evergreen conifer.

Next is a high-fired and glazed ceramic pot made in the United States. The flat round shape suits *bunjin* or literati-style plants. Choose a light, ethereal-appearing plant for best effect, such as a corokia, cotoneaster, or quince. Avoid a plant with pale blue flowers.

The third pot is a low, square brown container from China. Note the hand-painted drum-style border with rivets. This pot is designed for use with an accompaniment planting; that is, a small decorative grass, miniature bamboo, nandina, or flowering perennial. Mound the soil high, and display with a medium to large bonsai.

The fourth pot with yellow and brown stripes is an oval, glazed container from Japan. This is a classic *mame, shohin,* or miniature bonsai pot. Plant a woody deciduous tree or flowering evergreen in a container like this one. Chinese elm, miniature rose, dwarf pomegranate, or serissa would be nice.

The fifth pot is a low-fire glazed beige stoneware container of domestic manufacture. (See photo **1–1**, which is repeated below.) The thick square sides go best with a stout-trunk conifer. If possible, try to match the color of the pot and the trunk of the tree. Try a beige oak, cork-bark pine, or mountain hemlock.

1–1. Choose from these eleven pots one that will suit your bonsai.

The rather Victorian, oval-shape sixth pot is a low-fire glazed, cream-color container designed to complement miniature bulbs, mums, annuals, perennials, and delicate woody shrubs, such as the Arctic willow, birch, rosemary, and heather.

A classic cobalt-blue porcelain-glaze pot from China is the seventh. The color and shape are used widely for maples of all kinds, especially Japanese maples. Any woody tree or shrub with red fall color, red berries, or red fruit will look excellent in this container.

Here is an inexpensive plastic pot, the eighth in the photo, in the standard earth-brown color often seen with conifers. This type of container is primarily used as a training container for any developing or young bonsai. As the tree becomes a nice planting, it is transferred to a ceramic pot more worthy of bonsai.

A cascading pot, ninth in the photo, is in rich reds and blues over a base coat of dark gray glaze. This pot is locally made. Use a container like this for weeping, cascading, or extremely slanting flowering species—crab apple, quince, wild cherry, huckleberry, pyracantha, or hawthorn. For the best design, make sure to train a main lower branch to hang down over the edge of this pot.

Here is a round high-fired ceramic pot with blue glaze, tenth in the photo. The shape of this container from Japan is meant for a semi-cascading tree. A long lower branch should almost reach the surface of the table under the pot. Use twiggy plants with plenty of color in their fruits, nuts, seeds, or berries. Apricot, pistachio, plum, or dwarf citrus all hang nicely over the flared top edge of the pot.

And last in the photo (1–1) is the eleventh pot, a low-fired, terra-cotta antique container from China. Notice the fine mustard glaze and the artwork hand-painted on the side. This painting continues around the corners of the pot, making a large landscape with mountains, trees, and even boats in the bay. Because of the low firing, you want to use this pot indoors only, or it will crack. It would be perfect for a fig, dwarf schefflera, tea plant, or orange jasmine.

350-year-old pine in a nicely matching *tokoname*-ware Japanese pot. Admittedly, it looks quite nice, and it is one of my favorites. However, it requires watering three to four times a day in the summer. The pine needs the sun to be

1–2. 350-year-old pine in *tokoname*-ware pot.

SIZE

The size of the container is the single most important aspect of low-maintenance bonsai. The rules or conventions for traditional pot selection have been formed primarily by Japanese bonsai teachers who have attempted to train the eye of the inexperienced grower.

Most classical bonsai conform closely to the rule that the height of the pot is equal to the diameter of the trunk of the tree. See photo 1–2. This bonsai is a fine

healthy, so I cannot simply move it into the shade. This is a good example of a high-maintenance bonsai.

Similarly, 1–3 shows a remarkable 550-year-old maple, *Acer circi-*

1–3. 550-year-old maple (*Acer circinatum*).

1–4. Chinese elm (*Ulmus parviflora*).

modest size container slightly taller than the diameter of the trunk. This tree needs water only twice a day in the summer. But look at what happens when we repot it in an even larger container (**1–5**). For purposes of illustration, I have only placed the smaller pot inside the larger one. (For instructions on actual repotting, refer to chapter six.)

Back to our plant. If potted in this blue container, it would need water only once a day, even in the hottest weather. It would require even less on cool or cloudy days.

You could temporarily bring this tree into the house and safely spend a long weekend away at the beach.

natum. The small and shallow blue container does a good job of showing off the huge trunk on the tree and contrasts nicely with the reddish fall color of the leaves. I prefer the shocking underpotting of this old tree just to make it look more impressive and to test the horticultural limit of container growing.

While this can be done, again we create a high-maintenance bonsai. This tree, even in full shade, requires watering four times a day in the summer.

So what is the solution? Simply a bigger pot. In photo **1–4** you'll see a Chinese elm, *Ulmus parviflora,* in a

1–5. Chinese elm "repotted."

This is what I mean about pot size affecting the ease of maintaining your bonsai. The change in pot size in this case is insignificant for most hobby purposes.

The judges in a formal bonsai show might deduct some points for the oversize pot, but if that situation does not apply to you, who cares? A live tree in a big pot is better than a dead tree in the perfect-size container.

Here are some general rules of thumb about container size. Please note that temperature, wind, humidity, and the plant's vigor will affect these rules, so be aware of them. And, of course, your local climate will dictate care.

1–6. Japanese maple (*Acer palmatum*).

SHAPE

As you can see from the photo (**1–1** on pp. 9 and 10) and our discussion of eleven pots, there are many shapes of bonsai pots. The shape of a pot definitely alters the maintenance of the plant.

In **1–6** we see a Japanese maple, *Acer palmatum,* in a fairly small pot. The proportion of trunk size to height is nearly ideal; in fact, the trunk is actually slightly larger than the height of the pot. The problem with this container for the average grower is that the shape of the pot reduces the soil volume considerably. If you are trying to create a low-maintenance bonsai, avoid this shape.

Much of the height actually has no soil contained in it because of the legs of the pot. The shallow, oval shape contains far less soil than a rectangular pot of the same length would. Also, the curved sides take away additional soil volume. This beautiful container dries out in two hours in the summer, and it is more susceptible to freezing due to its large surface area and its legs. A cold wind can easily blow underneath the pot.

There are other shapes to avoid. Any pot that is narrower at the top opening than the sides makes it difficult to remove the root mass for repotting. This style can be found in all shapes and sizes of pots.

Look at the ninth pot in **1–1**. This cascading-style pot has a slight constriction at the top neck. This makes it extremely difficult to transplant any bonsai growing in it. You have to destroy many roots in order to extract the root ball from this type of container. This constriction is found in round, square, short, hexagonal, and rectangular pots as well. Be aware of this constriction and avoid these containers.

The literati-style container is another one to avoid. This miniature rhododendron, *Rhododendron impeditum*, is planted in a literati-style container (**1–7**). The second pot in **1–1** shows another. The small sides do not grip the soil mass well, and fairly tall and massive plants, like the rhododendron, have a tendency to pull out of the container in a strong wind. Also, the pot has only three legs, making it susceptible to tipping as well.

To make this plant into a low-maintenance

bonsai, prune down the height of the bonsai just a bit and plant it in a stout container similar to the seventh pot seen in **1–1**.

1–7. Miniature rhododendron (*Rhododendron impeditum*) in literati-style container.

1–8. Japanese green-mound juniper (*Juniperus procumbens* 'Nana') in a dark pot rapidly heats in summer.

COLOR

We are all familiar with the concepts of reflection and absorption. The lighter-colored containers reflect more of the sun's rays and therefore stay cooler. The juniper in **1–8** (on p. 14) is a Japanese green-mound juniper, *Juniperus procumbens* 'Nana,' planted in a traditional earth-brown container suitable to all conifers. The dark brown color and the lack of shiny glaze absorb the sun's rays very well. Only a flat black pot could absorb more.

1–9. Blue shimpaki juniper (*Juniperus chinensis* 'Blaauw'), when planted in a light-colored and shiny pot, means less summer watering.

This pot is so efficient at heating up in the summer that it must be watered three times a day in order to keep the juniper alive. If the bonsai were placed in the shade, the pot would stay cooler and the roots would retain moisture longer, but the sun-loving juniper would suffer.

The solution? A low-maintenance color, like that in **1–9** (below), shows a similar blue shimpaki juniper, *Juniperus chinensis* 'Blaauw.' I took advantage of the slightly blue foliage and matched it with a nice light blue-green glazed pot. The sun's rays are reflected quite a bit off the light color and doubly so because of the hard, shiny glaze. The resulting drop in temperature within the soil means I have to water this plant just once a day in the hottest weather.

MATERIALS

The Japanese maple, *Acer palmatum* in **1–10** (see p. 16), turns red in the frosty, clear days of early fall. If we had protected this tree indoors or in a greenhouse, we would not have gotten this nice rich red color.

Unfortunately, the containers most in use for bonsai will break apart during repeated freezing and thawing. This pot is made of high-fired porcelain clay. It does not absorb moisture like the low-fired clays, such as terra-cotta.

When a wet, low-fired clay freezes, it crumbles or pops apart, due to ice crystals expanding inside. The high-fired clay will withstand most freezes because it does not absorb very much moisture. Look for pots with a light cream or beige color to the inside clay. Some porcelains are almost white in color. Test the pot by flicking at it lightly with your fingernail. A good-quality pot will have a will immediately absorb the moisture like a thirsty sponge and show a considerable darkening in color when it is moist.

1–10. Japanese maple (*Acer palmatum*) in a high-fired porcelain clay pot, which does not absorb moisture and will not crack when frozen.

light, rather high-pitched ring to it. A low-quality clay will make a low-pitched "thunk" sound.

You can further test for clay quality by moistening a fingertip and applying it to the clay inside the pot. A high-quality container will be reluctant to absorb the moisture, and it will show only a minor change in color. A low-fired pot

In **1–11** (on p. 17) you'll see a Japanese larch, *Larix kaempferi*, in its golden fall color. The larch family loses its needles in winter just like the better-known deciduous maple, elm, and birch trees. With a bonsai, we are faced with a problem similar to that of the Japanese maple (**1–10**): to get good fall color, the plants must be subjected to some frost.

1–11. Japanese larch (*Larix kaempferi*) in mica pot that expands and contracts with heat and cold and, therefore, resists breakage.

Many dark bonsai pots are stoneware, and they can break during a sudden freezing spell when moist. This container is "plastic" and will not break. I use the word *plastic* in the sense that the material will give—expanding and contracting with heat and cold. Fired clay resists flexing and might break. This material is a mica pot of Korean manufacture. Not only are these containers good-looking, they are inexpensive and practically indestructible. They definitely qualify as low-maintenance pots.

Other materials that are resistant to cracking and breaking are fiberglass, hypertuffa, and plain rock slabs used as pots. Try a forest planting on a flat rock. The trees are

1–12. Perhaps the world's oldest deciduous bonsai. This collected vine maple (*Acer circinatum*) specimen is estimated to be over 1,200 years old.

easy to assemble into a group when young. In time, the roots clasp the rock and make a nice natural scene.

The venerable old bonsai, a vine maple, *Acer circinatum* (**1–12** above), estimated to be over 1,200 years old, demonstrates the painstaking care of bonsai growers through the centuries. But don't let this monument of diligence and loving care inhibit you from creating and maintaining your own pleasing low-maintenance bonsai in your garden or window in just a few years—or indeed in a single growing season.

Chapter Two
PLANTS

2–1. Japanese maple (*Acer palmatum* 'Ezono Momiji').

GENERAL CONSIDERATIONS

Obviously, choosing the right plant can make a difference in the amount of time you care for it. Some plants are naturally low-maintenance species, and others are very high maintenance. Your personal enjoyment of the task of caring for a plant can easily turn a high-maintenance species into a labor of love and therefore increase growing success as well. I know many orchid growers who simply have no idea of the time they spend in their greenhouses; they are lost in their own little worlds. Bonsai growers can be like that, too. Still, there are low-maintenance plants. Some plants seem to thrive on neglect. Jade trees can go months without water. Native plants from your local area survive well both in summer and winter. Other plants are tolerant of low light, drought, or subzero temperatures.

Assess your personal growing style, climate, work schedule, vacation habits, and desire to nurture a plant. Look over lists of plants recommended for bonsai to find a good match for you. The lowest-maintenance bonsai you can grow will be the one with the right combination of hardy species, appropriate growing conditions, and your love for the plant. Make your choices with care.

In this chapter, you'll find photos of a sweet gum, a photinia, and some of my favorite maples in glorious fall colors (**2–1** to **2–16**).

INDOORS OR OUT?

Well-meaning individuals try to grow juniper bonsai on their coffee tables. A pine tree slowly withers on top of the television set. A florist azalea turns black on the picnic table outside. These sad occurrences don't have to happen.

If you buy a bonsai, pay careful attention to the location in which it was growing. Most florist shops sell indoor bonsai. Most garden nurseries sell outdoor bonsai. If there is any question at all, feel free to ask the shopkeeper. Additional growing information is usually provided as a handout, brochure, or instruction label. Read these materials very carefully. If there are still any questions in your mind, contact one of the members of your local bonsai society or garden club.

With recent burgeoning interest in bonsai comes a variety of available bonsai . . . not all of them real. Bonsai can now be found that are made of silk, paper, silver wire, plastic, and other sturdy materials. A new product, quite convincing in appearance, is a preserved plant. Typically a juniper, this bonsai look-alike can be quite green and flexible and may be planted in a plastic bonsai container. A naïve customer or gift recipient might actually believe that this plant will thrive and grow.

2–2. Tana maple (*Acer palmatum* 'Tana').

2–3. Full-Moon Maple (*Acer japonicum* 'Acontifolium').

With a variety of shops supplying bonsai and bonsai material, it becomes imperative that the purchaser get a positive identification of the plant.

If the identity isn't known, it will also be difficult to know how to care for the plant. I've seen bonsai for sale at outdoor markets, grocery stores, department stores, and variety shops. In these establishments, the bonsai might have been placed on a shelf only temporarily; the plant's surroundings may not indicate the best environment for successfully growing it.

Avoid using common names. A Norfolk Island pine isn't really a pine; a Hinoki cypress isn't a cypress; a Chinese snow rose isn't a rose. The common name for a plant is sometimes misleading, and it may vary regionally. Most serious gardeners use the plant's Latin or scientific name. To ensure accurate information, I'll refer to the Latin name wherever practical.

You'll find plant lists of "Suggested Outdoor Bonsai" (pp. 25–35) and "Suggested Indoor Bonsai" (pp. 36–37), with common and scientific names that include most of the larger groups of plants suitable for bonsai.

Consider these partial lists; we could not possibly include all suitable plants, only the more common ones. These lists are alphabetized by scientific name and are by no means complete. Most bonsai plants can be grouped into one of three environmental classifications: indoor bonsai, outdoor bonsai, and partially outdoor bonsai.

ABOUT INDOOR BONSAI

Indoor bonsai are made from tropical plants. Florist shops sell these indoor plants that are native to the tropical regions of Africa, Asia, and South America. Small-leaf varieties are most often suggested due to the enormous size of leaves found in plants of these lush regions. The bonsai are usually placed in a well-lit location that has adequate ventilation. In warmer climates, these bonsai may be brought outside for a limited time in full shade.

Some plants often used include figs, schefflera, *Aralia cycas,* kalanchoe, pelargonium, succulents, cacti, portulacaria, hibiscus, fatshedera, crassula, hedera, nerium, pilea, poinsettia, and bougainvillea.

2–4. American sweet gum (*Liquidamber styraciflua* 'Gamboll').

2–5. Japanese maple from seed (*Acer palmatum*).

ABOUT OUTDOOR BONSAI

Outdoor bonsai are typically conifers, broad-leafed evergreens, and deciduous trees native to colder climates. These hardy trees and shrubs are subject to freezing temperatures every winter in their natural habitats. As bonsai, they will tolerate some freezing temperatures overnight.

The variety of plants in this classification is large, accounting for most bonsai species. Included are pine, juniper, hemlock, spruce, fir, cedar, rhododendron, azalea, alder, hornbeam, birch, beech, camellia, quince, dogwood, redbud, cypress, hawthorn, larch, filbert, cherry, pear, oak, willow, and arborvitae.

ABOUT PARTIALLY OUTDOOR BONSAI

Partially outdoor bonsai are native to temperate climates. While they may sometimes freeze in their local environment, these potted trees need not be subjected to cold temperatures.

Typically, a bonsai grower will move the plant about as the seasons dictate. Place the bonsai in the shade outdoors in April. The plant can spend the summer cooling in the breezes under the canopy of a large tree. When the first frosts arrive, the tree can become an indoor bonsai, in a sunny location in the home.

Some good examples of these plants are evergreen oak, evergreen maple, Chinese elm, Japanese green-mound juniper, Kingsbury boxwood, Chinese tea, pomegranate, bamboo, Montezuma cypress, bald cypress, buttonwood (sycamore), fuchsia, magnolia, olive, palm, Seiju elm, Hokkaido elm, Chinese snow rose, and Chinese date tree.

I hope this brief overview will correct a common misconception. Most bonsai exhibitions are found indoors—in convention centers, malls, and art galleries. Unfortunately, many beginners to the horticulture of bonsai start off thinking that all bonsai are indoor plants. Indeed, this is where bonsai trees look fabulous. However, most bonsai are outdoor plants.

If you must have an indoor bonsai, simply pot and train an indoor plant. If you purchase a finished bonsai, be aware of its needs. A tropical plant doesn't have to feel the seasons, since there are none in its native habitat. Such a plant only needs lots of indirect light, consistent moisture, and moderate heat.

Most outdoor temperate-zone plants need to feel the passage of the seasons in order to set their internal biological clocks. These plants depend heavily on the height, location, and duration of the sun to create winter, spring, summer, and fall, just as all plants do that are native to colder climates. If you satisfy the needs of the plants, the bonsai will satisfy you in return.

2–6. Trident maple (*Acer buergeranum*).

SUGGESTED OUTDOOR BONSAI

Abies amabilis	Pacific Silver Fir (Cascade Fir)
Abies balsamea 'Nana'	Dwarf Balsam Fir
Abies koreana	Korean Fir
Abies lasiocarpa	Alpine Fir
Abies lasiocarpa 'Arizonica'	Cork Fir
Acer buergeranum	Trident Maple
Acer campestre	Hedge Maple (Field Maple)
Acer campestre 'Compactum'	Compact Hedge Maple
Acer capillipes	Japanese Red Maple
Acer circinatum	Vine Maple
Acer ginnala	Amur Maple
Acer griseum	Paperbark Maple
Acer japonicum	Full-Moon Maple (Japanese Maple)
Acer japonicum 'Aconitifolium'	Lace-Leaf Full-Moon Maple
Acer japonicum 'Auerum'	Golden Full-Moon Maple
Acer oblongum	Evergreen Maple
Acer palmatum	Japanese Maple

2–7. Japanese maple (*Acer palmatum* 'Varigatum Dissectum').

2–8. Paperbark maple (*Acer griseum*).

Acer palmatum 'Arakawa'	Arakawa Japanese Maple
Acer palmatum 'Butterfly'	Japanese Butterfly Maple
Acer palmatum 'Kiyo Hime'	Kiyo Hime Japanese Maple
Acer palmatum 'Koshimino'	Dwarf Japanese Maple
Acer palmatum 'Linearilobum'	Thread-Leaf Maple
Acer palmatum 'Sangokaku'	Coral-Bark Maple
Acer palmatum 'Shishigashira'	Dwarf Japanese Maple
Acer paxii	Lobed Evergreen Maple
Acer rubrum	Red Maple (Scarlet Maple, Soft Maple, Swamp Maple)
Acer saccharinum grandidentatum	Silver Maple (White Maple, River Maple)
Acer tataricum	Tatarian Maple
Acer truncatum	Chinese Maple (Shantung Maple)
Albizia julibrissin	Mimosa (Silk Tree)

Alnus tenuifolia	Mountain Alder
Arctostaphylos manzanita	Manzanita (Parry Maple)
Arundinaria disticha	Dwarf Fern-Leaf Bamboo
Arundinaria marmorea	Dwarf Black Bamboo
Betula 'Nana'	Dwarf Arctic Birch
Betula pendula 'Laciniata'	Cut-Leaf Weeping Birch (European White Birch)
Betula pendula 'Fastigiata'	Pyramidal White Birch
Betula pendula 'Purpurea'	Purple Birch
Betula pendula 'Trost's Dwarf'	Trost's Dwarf Birch
Betula platyphylla 'Japonica'	Japanese White Birch
Buxus microphylla 'Compacta'	Dwarf Boxwood
Buxus microphylla 'Koreana'	Korean Boxwood
Buxus microphylla 'Morris Midget'	Morris Midget Boxwood
Calocedrus decurrens 'Compacta'	California Incense Cedar
Camellia sasanqua	Sasanqua Camellia
Camellia sinensis	Tea Plant (Sweet Camellia)
Camellia vernalis	Vernalis Camellia
Caprinus betulus	European Hornbeam (European Ironwood)
Carpinus caroliniana	American Hornbeam (Blue Beech, Water Beech)
Carpinus turczaninovii	Turkish Hornbeam
Cedrus brevifolia	Cyprus Cedar
Cedrus libani	Cedar-of-Lebanon

2–9. Japanese maple (*Acer palmatum* 'Flavescens').

Cedrus libani 'Nana'	Dwarf Cedar-of-Lebanon
Celtis sinensis	Japanese Hackberry
Cercis chinensis	Chinese Redbud (Chinese Judas Tree)
Cercocarpus ledifolius	Curl-Leaf Mountain Mahogany
Chaenomeles japonica	Japanese Flowering Quince
Chamaecyparis lawsoniana	Lawson Cypress (Port Orford Cedar)
Chamaecyparis lawsoniana 'Ellwoodii Improved'	Ellwood Cypress
Chamaecyparis lawsoniana 'Minima Glauca'	Dwarf Blue Cypress
Chamaecyparis nootkatensis 'Compacta'	Dwarf Alaska Cedar (Nootkatensis Cypress)
Chamaecyparis obtusa 'Filicoides'	Hinoki Cypress (Hinoki False Cypress, Fernspray Cypress)
Chamaecyparis obtusa 'Kosteri'	Koster Cypress (Hinoki Cypress)
Chamaecyparis obtusa 'Nana'	Dwarf Hinoki Cypress
Chamaecyparis pisifera	Sawara Cypress
Chamaecyparis pisifera 'Filifera'	Threadlike Cypress
Chamaecyparis thyoides 'Andelyensis Conica'	White Cedar (Southern White Cedar, Swamp White Cedar)
Chrysanthemum morifolium	Florist's Chrysanthemum (Mum)
Clematis montana Anemone Clematis	(Virgin's Bower, Leather Flower, Vase Vine)
Coffea arabica	Arabian Coffee
Cornus kousa	Korean Dogwood (Kousa, Kousa Dogwood, Kousa Cornel)

2–10. Japanese maple with seeds (*Acer palmatum* 'Summinagashi').

Cornus mas or *Cornus mascula*	Cornelian Cherry
Corokia cotoneaster	Corokia
Corylus avellana 'Contorta'	European Filbert (European Hazel, Hazelnut, Harry Lauder's Walking Stick)
Corylus colurna	Turkish Hazelnut (Turkish Filbert)
Corylus maxima 'Purpurea'	Giant Purple Filbert
Cotoneaster congestus	Dwarf Cotoneaster
Cotoneaster microphyllus 'Thymifolius'	Dwarf Thyme-Leaf Cotoneaster
Crassula argentea 'Crosby's Dwarf'	Dwarf Jade Tree (Dwarf Rubber Plant)
Crassula tetragona	Miniature Pine (Baby-Pine-of-China, Chinese Pine)
Crataegus ambigua	Russian Hawthorn (Russian Thorn Apple, Russian Haw)
Cryptomeria japonica 'Bandai Sugi'	Conical Cryptomeria (Japanese Cedar)
Cryptomeria japonica 'Jindai-sugi'	Globular Cryptomeria (Japanese Cedar)
Cryptomeria japonica 'Pygmaea'	Dwarf Cryptomeria (Dwarf Japanese Cedar)
Cryptomeria japonica 'Tansu'	Tansu Cryptomeria
Cupressus forbesii	Telcate Cypress
Cupressus macrolarpa	Monterey Cypress
Eurya emarginata 'Microphylla'	Japanese Fern Tree
Fagus sylvatica 'Asplenifolia'	Oak-Leaf European Beech
Fagus sylvatica 'Atropurpurea'	Copper European Beech
Fagus sylvatica 'Lanciniata'	Cut-Leaf Beech (Fern-Leaf Beech)

2–11. This broadleaf evergreen, photinia (*Photinia fraseri*), shows new red growth in spring.

2–12. Japanese maple (*Acer palmatum* 'Mizu Kurguri').

Fagus sylvatica 'Rohanii'	Purple Cut-Leaf Beech (Purple Fern-Leaf Beech)
Fagus sylvatica 'Spathiana'	Yellow Beech
Fagus sylvatica 'Tricolor'	Tricolor Beech
Fagus sylvatica 'Zlatia'	Golden Beech
Fortunella margarita 'Nagami'	Nagami Kumquat
Fuchsia magellanica 'Isis'	Fuchsia
Ginkgo biloba	Maidenhair Tree
Grevillea rosmarinifolia	Spider Flower (Rosemary Tree)
Hakea macra 'Aureola'	Japanese Forest Grass
Hamamelis mollis	Chinese Witch Hazel
Ilex crenata 'Mariesii'	Dwarf Japanese Holly (Dwarf Box-Leaved Holly)
Ilex dimorpophylla	Okinawan Holly
Imperata cylindrica 'Rubra'	Japanese Blood Grass
Juniperus chinensis 'Parsonii'	Prostrate Juniper
Juniperus chinensis 'Procumbens Nana'	Dwarf Japanese Juniper
Juniperus chinensis 'Sargentii' or 'Shimpaki'	Shimpaki (Pyramidal Japanese Juniper)
Juniperus chinensis 'Blaauw'	Blue Shimpaki
Juniperus chinensis 'Torulosa'	Hollywood Juniper
Juniperus chinensis 'Skyrocket'	Skyrocket Juniper
Juniperus communis 'Compressa'	Dwarf Columnar Juniper

2–13. Autumn moon maple (*Acer japonicum* 'Aureum').

Juniperus squamata 'Blue Star'	Blue Star Juniper
Larix decidua	European Larch
Larix kaempferi	Japanese Larch
Magnolia parviflora or *Magnolia sieboldii*	Oyama Magnolia
Malus 'Dorothea'	Yellow Crab Apple (pink flowers)
Malus 'Radiant'	Red Crab Apple (red flowers)
Malus zumi calocarpa	Red Crab Apple (white flowers)
Malus floribunda	Japanese Flowering Crab Apple (Showy Crab Apple, Purple Chokeberry)
Miscanthus sacchariflorus	Amur Silver Grass
Myrtus communis 'Microphylla'	Dwarf Myrtle
Narcissus asturiensis or *Narcissus minimus*	Dwarf Daffodil
Narcissus triandrus	Angel's Tears Daffodil
Nothofagus antarctica	Antarctic Beech
Olea europaea 'Little Ollie'	Dwarf Olive
Parrotia persica	Persian Beech
Phoenix roebelenii	Pygmy Date Palm (Roebelin Palm, Miniature Date Palm)
Photinia fraseri	Photinia
Picea abies 'Mucronata'	Dwarf Norway Spruce
Picea abies 'Pygmaea'	Pygmy Norway Spruce

2–14. Japanese maple (*Acer palmatum* 'Sekimori').

2–15. Red maple (*Acer rubrum scalpendolium* 'Gable').

Picea engelmannii	Engelmann Spruce
Picea glauca 'Conica'	Dwarf White Spruce (Cat Spruce, Dwarf Alberta Spruce)
Pieris japonica 'Compacta'	Dwarf Andromeda (Dwarf Lily-of-the-Valley Bush)
Pinus albicaulis	White-Bark Pine
Pinus aristata	Bristle-Cone Pine (Hickory Pine)
Pinus balfouriana	Foxtail Pine
Pinus bungeana	Lace-Bark Pine
Pinus cembroides 'Monophylla'	Mexican Stone Pine
Pinus contorta 'Murrayana'	Lodgepole Pine (Shore Pine, Beach Pine)
Pinus densiflora	Japanese Red Pine
Pinus densiflora 'Umbraculifera'	Tanyosho Pine (Japanese Umbrella Pine)
Pinus edulis	Pinyon Pine (Nut Pine, Two-Leaved Nut Pine)
Pinus flexilis	Limber Pine
Pinus halepensis	Aleppo Pine (Jerusalem Pine)
Pinus monophylla	Single-Leaf Pinyon Pine (Nut Pine, Stone Pine)
Pinus monticola	Western White Pine
Pinus mugo 'Mugo'	Dwarf Mugo Pine (Mountain Pine)
Pinus nigra	Austrian Pine
Pinus pinea	Italian Stone Pine (Umbrella Pine, Stone Pine)
Pinus strobus	Eastern White Pine
Pinus strobus 'Nana'	Dwarf Eastern White Pine
Pinus sylvestris 'Nana'	Dwarf Scotch Pine (Dwarf Scotch Fir, Scots Pine)
Pinus thunbergiana	Japanese Black Pine
Pistacia chinensis	Chinese Pistachio
Platanus occidentalis	Eastern Sycamore (Eastern Buttonwood, American Plane Tree)
Podocarpus nivalis	Alpine Yew
Populus tremuloides	Quaking Aspen (Trembling Aspen, Quiverleaf)
Potentilla fruticosa	Shrubby Cinquefoil (Golden Hardhack, Widdy)
Prunus serrulata 'Hally Jollivette'	Pink Flowering Cherry
Prunus serrulata	Japanese Flowering Cherry (Oriental Cherry)
Prunus cistena	Purple-Leaf Sand Cherry
Prunus mume	Japanese Flowering Apricot
Prunus tomentosa	Nanking Cherry (Hansen's Bush Cherry, Chinese Bush Fruit)

Prunus virginiana	Chokecherry
Pseudolarix kaempferi	Golden Larch
Punica granatum 'Nana'	Dwarf Pomegranate
Pyracantha coccinea 'Red Elf'	Compact Fire Thorn
Pyrus kawakamii	Evergreen Pear
Pyrus salicifolia 'Pendula'	Willow-Leaved Pear
Quercus dumosa	California Scrub Oak
Quercus ilex	Holly Oak (Holm Oak)
Quercus myrsinifolia	Japanese Evergreen Oak
Quercus phellos	Willow Oak
Quercus suber	Cork Oak
Quercus vacciniifolia	Huckleberry Oak
Rhododendron 'Blue Diamond'	Rhododendron (Azalea, lavender flowers)
Rhododendron 'Bow Bells'	Rhododendron (Azalea, pink flowers)

2–16. Trident maple (*Acer buergeranum*).

Rhododendron 'Ginny Gee'	Rhododendron (Azalea, pink to white flowers)
Rhododendron 'Hotel'	Rhododendron (Azalea, yellow flowers)
Rhododendron kiusianum	Kyushu Azalea
Rhododendron mucronulatum	Deciduous Purple Azalea
Rhododendron 'Nancy Evans'	Orange Azalea
Rhododendron 'Trilby'	Red Azalea
Rhododendron 'Satsuki Hybrids'	Satsuki Azalea (many colors)
Rhododendron 'Kurume Hybrids'	Kurume Azalea (many colors)
Rhodohypoxis baurii	Dwarf Rhodohypoxis Bulbs
Salix purpurea 'Nana'	Dwarf Purple Osier (Dwarf Basket Willow)
Salix sachalinensis 'Sekka' or 'Setsuka'	Setsuka Willow
Schefflera arboricola	Umbrella Tree (Rubber Tree, Starleaf, Hawaiian Elf Schefflera)
Serissa foetida	Japanese Snow Rose
Sorbus reducta	Dwarf Mountain Ash
Sorbus tianshanica	Turkestan Mountain Ash
Styrax japonicus	Japanese Snowbell
Syringa koreana	Korean Lilac
Taxodium distichum	Bald Cypress
Taxodium mucronatum	Montezuma Cypress
Taxus cuspidata 'Nana'	Dwarf Japanese Yew
Taxus media 'Brownii'	Brown's Yew
Thuja occidentalis 'Little Gem'	Little Gem Arborvitae (American Arborvitae, White Cedar)
Thuja occidentalis 'Nana'	Dwarf American Arborvitae (Dwarf White Cedar)
Tilia cordata	Small-Leafed European Linden (Basswood, Lime Tree, Whitewood)
Tsuga canadensis 'Redula'	Weeping Canada Hemlock (Hemlock Spruce)
Ulmus parvifolia	Chinese Elm
Ulmus parvifolia 'Hokkaido'	Chinese Elm (Hokkaido Elm)
Ulmus parvifolia 'Seiju'	Seiju Elm
Wisteria floribunda	Japanese Wisteria
Wisteria sinensis	Chinese Wisteria
Zelkova serrata	Saw-Leaf Zelkova (Japanese Zelkova)
Ziziphus jujuba	Chinese Date Tree (Common Jujube, Chinese Jujube)

Suggested Indoor Bonsai

Acacia baileyana	Acacia (Cootamundra Wattle, Golden Mimosa)
Acacia julibrissin or *Albizia julibrissin*	Acacia
Araucaria heterophylla 'Excelsa'	Araucaria Pine (Norfolk Island Pine, Australian Pine, House Pine)
Ardisia crenata	Coralberry, Spiceberry
Bambusa glaucescens	Hedge Bamboo (Oriental Hedge Bamboo)
Bougainvillea glabra	Lesser Bougainvillea (Paper Flower)
Bucida spinosa	Dwarf Black Olive
Buddleia davidii	Summer Lilac (Orange-Eye Butterfly Bush)
Bursera simaruba	West Indian Birch (Gumbo-Limbo, Gum Elemi)
Calliandra species	Powderpuff
Carissa grandifolia	Natal Plum (Amatungulu)
Cassia marilandica	Wild Senna
Chamaecyparis pisifera 'Plumosa'	Sawara Cypress (False Cypress, conical)
Chamaecyparis pisifera 'Nana'	Dwarf Sawara Cypress
Chamaecyparis pisifera 'Squarrosa'	Sawara Cypress (dense)
Chrysanthemum frutescens	Marguerite (White Marguerite, Paris Daisy)
Cinnamomum camphora	Camphor Tree
Coffea arabica	Arabian Coffee (Common Coffee, Arabica Coffee)
Coffea robusta or *Coffea canephora*	Robusta Coffee (Wild Robusta Coffee)
Cotoneaster microphyllus	Cotoneaster
Cotoneaster microphyllus 'Cochleatus'	Dwarf Cotoneaster
Cuphea hyssopifolia	False Heather (Elfin Herb)
Cytisus racemosus	Broom
Eugenia brasiliensis	Brazil Cherry (Grumichama, Grumixameira)
Eurya japonica	Japanese Elderberry (Japanese Eurya)
Ficus caria	Fig Tree
Fortunella margarita or *Fortunella hindsii*	Kumquat
Fuchsia megllanica or *Fuchsia gracilis*	Hardy Fuchsia
Guaiacum officinale	Pockwood Tree (Lignum-vitae)
Hedera helix	English Ivy

Hibiscus rosa-sinensis	Blacking Plant (Chinese Hibiscus, Hawaiian Hibiscus, Rose-of-China, China Rose)
Hibiscus tiliaceus	Lagoon Hibiscus (Mahoe)
Holarrhena antidysenteria	Holarrhena
Ilex crenata	Japanese Holly (Box-Leaved Holly)
Ixora coccinea or *Ixora incarnata*	Jungle Geranium
Ixora javanica	Asian Ixora
Leptospermum scoparium	Tea Tree (New Zealand Tea Tree, Manuka)
Ligustrum japonicum	Japanese Privet (Wax-Leaf Privet)
Ligustrum japonicum rotundifolium	Round-Leaf Japanese Privet
Lonicera nitida	Chinese Honeysuckle
Nothofagus cunninghamii	Tasmanian Beech
Pelargonium species	Geranium
Pistacia vera	Pistachio
Pittosporum tobira	Japanese Pittosporum (Australian Laurel, Mock Orange, House Blooming Mock Orange)
Psidium cattleianum	Strawberry Guava
Pyracantha species	Fire Thorn
Quercus suber	Cork Oak
Raphiolepis indica	Indian Hawthorn
Rosmarinus offficinalis	Rosemary
Taxodium distichum	Bald Cypress (deciduous)
Trachelospermum jasminoides	Star Jasmine (Confederate Jasmine)
Wrightia species	Wrightia

RECOMMENDED PLANTS FOR BEGINNERS

Top Ten Outdoor Plants

These are excellent outdoor plants: (1) all junipers, especially 'Procumbens,' 'Nana,' and 'Shimpaki'; (2) all maples, especially Japanese, red, amur, and trident maple; (3) all Chinese elms; (4) most mountain pines, especially mugo pine, Japanese black pine, and Japanese white pine; (5) all *Larix* (larch) species; (6) *Malus,* any small-leaf crab apple species; (7) *Taxodium distichum* (bald cypress); (8) *Zelkova,* all varieties; (9) all hawthorn; and (10) quince.

Outdoor Plants to Avoid

Avoid using these plants for outdoor bonsai: (1) spruce; (2) walnut; (3) oak; (4) ash; (5) *Chamaecyparis* (false cypress); (6) *Cryptomeria* (Japanese cedar); (7) birch; (8) beech; (9) willow; and (10) ginkgo.

Top Ten Indoor Plants

These are excellent indoor plants: (1) *Ficus* (fig), any small-leaf variety; (2) dwarf schefflera; (3) dwarf pomegranate; (4) *Olea* (olive) species; (5) orange jasmine; (6) *Serissa foetida;* (7) buttonwood (sycamore); (8) bougainvillea; (9) *Bucida* species (dwarf black olive); and (10) *Camellia sinensis* (tea plant, sweet camellia).

2-17. This Chinese elm tree (*Ulmus parvifolia,* left) makes a good outdoor bonsai plant, but beginners should avoid beech trees like this specimen (*Fagus sylvatica,* right).

2-18. Zelkova (*Zelkova serrata*), like this one which is showing off its fall color, grows well outdoors.

2-19. A common juniper (*Juniperus communis*) makes an excellent outdoor bonsai.

2-20. This Japanese maple (*Acer palmatum*), grown from seed, is 36 years old.

CHAPTER THREE

SOIL

3–1. Screen for sifting soil.

BONSAI SOIL

Experienced bonsai growers know the value of a good bonsai soil. It drains well, preventing rot, fungus, and disease. It does not trap moisture, which prevents roots from being damaged during freezing weather, but it retains sufficient moisture to protect the roots during unseasonable hot spells. It packs easily during transplanting to avoid air pockets in the soil, yet it remains loose to allow healthy air flow. It has the correct pH for the plants' roots. It will not decompose or condense into soggy clay in the bonsai container.

A good bonsai soil is plant insurance for your bonsai. It will work hard for you and make your job easier. Among beginners, poor bonsai soil accounts for a great many deaths of bonsai. Successful and low-maintenance growing depends on a proper growing medium. There are special conditions in a bonsai pot that are not found in the ground—not even in a normal flowerpot.

Particle Size

Normal soil from the garden is unsuitable for use in containers of any kind. Commercially bagged potting soil is better, but it still is not the best. Any potting soil can be made into excellent bonsai soil, however, by simply running it through a common window screen. Throw away all the dust and small stuff that passes through. The bonsai soil is what remains on top of the screen. Wet soil does not screen very well, so dry the soil in the sun or inside the house before screening it. Some potting soils contain a lot of large chunks of bark or pumice. Either hand-pick those out or screen them out with a one-fourth-inch hardware cloth or soffit screen found at any hardware store. Simple wooden frames can be made to support a square foot of screen, or soil sieves can be purchased at bonsai nurseries (3–1; see p. 41).

Particle size is very important. I know that this screening business seems like an inconvenient and laborious task. But good bonsai soil guarantees the health of your plant.

Soil Components

Every plant has an ideal soil mix that will promote optimum growth and health. Azaleas prefer growing in leaf litter, organic compost, or ground-up bark chips. Apple trees prefer a rather rocky, poor soil. We go up to the mountain to observe junipers clinging to life from a rocky ledge. We see cacti growing in soil that's practically all sand.

Each species has its own optimal blend of organic and inorganic components in its soil. For best results in growing bonsai, we try to duplicate the natural soil conditions under which the plant would be growing in its native environment.

Organic components are soil particles that have been alive at one time. Sometimes organic can imply "grown in the absence of pesticides," but I am using the term *organic* to mean "carbon-based compounds that were formerly alive." This includes leaf litter, ground bark, sawdust, or cedar shavings, as well as other plant remains. Wild manures, such as those from range steer, bison, or moose, are suitable as organic components because their main ingredient is chopped straw. Avoid fresh barnyard manures as a soil component. They are too difficult to screen and they compact too easily. See chapter ten for their use as fertilizers.

Inorganic components are non-living rock or mineral products. Some examples are decomposed granite, turkey or chicken grit, perlite, vermiculite pumice, sharp masons' sand, finely ground gravel, lava cinders, or smashed clay pots. Kitty litter can be use if it contains no deodorant, and the clay particles used to pick up oil spills on your garage floor will work as well. Commercially available fired clay particles come with many names: akadama, Terra-Green, Isolite, Haydite, and many others. They are all suitable.

The serious bonsai grower keeps handy one bin of screened organic particles and another separate bin of screened inorganic soil. During potting or repotting you can simply custom-mix your soil to fit the species of plant. Below are some general guidelines to help you mix the right proportion of each, according to the plant.

Some of the major genera are listed in five groups, as examples to help guide you to correct soil mixing. This plant list is by no means complete. Getting the composition exactly right is not so critical, because particle size is actually more important than the pH.

MICROORGANISMS

Fertile soil is never sterile. The word *sterile,* though, is sometimes used commercially to indicate weed-free; a bag of potting soil will often tout the word *sterile* as reassurance that this bag contains good stuff, not bad stuff. If the soil really were sterile, it would house no bacteria, no spores, no seed, no mold, no fungi, no viruses, no insects, no eggs, no larvae, etc. When potting soil is labeled sterile, the suppliers mean that it is not likely to contain insects and disease.

Many plants take advantage of microorganisms to accomplish life processes. Fertile soil is full of microorganisms. Many forms of bacteria contribute to the breakdown of soil. The effects are quite beneficial and contribute to what soil scientists call ion exchange. Excellent ion exchange is associated with a superior soil. Poor ion exchange indicates a lack of important chemical interactions, resulting in reduced nutrient exchange, limited moisture uptake, and, in general, a slowing down of the biochemistry that supports the life of the plant.

PLANTS AND RECOMMENDED SOILS

Group 1—Azalea, rhododendron, bald cypress, redwood, tropical foliage plants. Use three-fourths organic and one-fourth inorganic.

Group 2—Alder, birch, beech, hornbeam, elm, zelkova, dogwood, maple. Use two-thirds organic and one-third inorganic.

Group 3—Pyracantha, wisteria, quince, fig, corokia, holly, boxwood, apple, peach, pear, cherry, plum, cotoneaster. Use one-half organic and one-half inorganic.

Group 4—Larch, ginkgo, fir, spruce, hemlock, cypress, cryptomeria. Use one-third organic and two-thirds inorganic.

Group 5—Oak, pine, juniper, alpine and desert plant, jade, eucalyptus. Use one-fourth organic and three-fourths inorganic.

Avoid any soil that has weeds growing in it. Also do not use roadside soil, beach sand or soil, river sand, manures, high-mineral soil, discarded soil, used or deodorized kitty litter, aquarium gravel, or fine peat moss, since they contain components you want to avoid.

Roadside Soil—This may contain asphalt residues, pesticides, and dust, which are difficult to wash out. There will be no beneficial bacteria.

Beach Sand or Soils—They contain salt and other minerals, and washing them out is inefficient and the job incomplete.

River Sand—The edges have been polished smooth over time; there are no beneficial cracks and crevices for roots, moisture, nutrients, or helpful bacteria.

Manures as Soil—They may contain straw and undigested organic material, but the remaining time that these will stay firm and particulate is limited. They will break down completely and soil compaction will result. A manure slurry fertilizer, however, is beneficial, and manure as a soil amendment is fine.

High-Mineral Soil—Beware because these have often been formed as the result of sedimentation of alkali or brackish lake beds in high desert areas.

Discarded Soil—It is tempting to reuse potting soil, but I cannot recommend it. Why didn't the former plant do well? What was the former plant treated with in its lifetime? Perhaps nothing, but possibly insecticides, fungicides, nonutilized fertilizers, and more. It is best to start fresh.

Used Kitty Litter—Even though you screen out the solid waste, the urine does not wash out easily or completely.

Deodorized Kitty Litter—The little blue or green particles in this type of kitty litter contain dyes and fragrances that affect soil performance in a negative way.

Aquarium Gravel—These gravels are highly polished, which is bad . . . or artificially colored, which is worse . . . , and they may be coated with a substance to make them attractive under black lights.

Fine Peat Moss—This material is nitrogen-starved. It will rob nitrogen from the plant faster than you can fertilize. When the nitrogen is finally at a level high enough for the material, it is then too high for the plant. A scum forms on the surface of the soil, blocking air and interfering with watering and drainage. Use only dark, well-rotted, and stabilized wood products. I prefer hemlock bark for its lack of slivers.

CHAPTER FOUR

TRAINING

4–1. Rhododendron in fall; in late spring use pruning method G.

WHY WE SHAPE BONSAI

All plants grow differently when they are young versus when they are older. They grow at different rates of speed—faster when young. As the foliage begins to mature and harden, the branch structure changes from an obscure, generalized "shrubby" shape to one of delineated refinement. The horizontal branches and spaces between them are a visual signal to us that the tree is more mature. We try to copy the effect from nature on bonsai in order to make our little trees seem older and more refined. We revere and appreciate the older, weathered shapes and try to copy their styles.

There are perhaps seventy different styles of bonsai, and each has its own individual shaping concerns. A complete description of these would be inappropriate for this book. For a more detailed treatment of those issues, the interested reader is encouraged to consult an advanced text, such as my book *Keep Your Bonsai Perfectly Shaped* (Sterling, 1997).

4–2. Copper-clad aluminum wire is used to spread out branches of this hemlock tree.

SHAPING WITH WIRE

COILED WIRE

Perhaps the most widely practiced shaping technique is the use of copper or aluminum wire to bend branches (4–2 above). The hemlock branches of the tree in the photo needed to be spread out from each other. They were loosely wound with copper-clad aluminum wire, then bent into position. The wires can be removed after one year, and the branches will remain in place.

Be sure to cut off the wire. Do not attempt to unwind the wire; you risk damaging the branch. Notice that the wire has plenty of space between it and the live branch. This is to ensure room for the branch to grow. A wire that is placed too tightly will strangle the branch and create an unsightly coiled scar.

THE PULL-DOWN METHOD

The lower branches on this elm (4–3, opposite on p. 47) needed to be pulled down to separate them from the upper part of the tree. A small-gauge wire was inserted under one of the tree's roots and secured with a few twists. Then the top end of the wire was fastened around the freshly lowered branch while the wire was twisted around it in its new position.

These branches did not require a lot of force. If you are pulling on a branch with a lot of resistance, it would be advisable to protect the branches and roots with a wrap of floral tape. Simply wind the floral tape a few times around the branch where the wire will be attached. This will keep the wire from cutting into the branch. For minor pulls, this is not necessary.

4–3. Pulling down lower branches of elm tree. Chinks in the wire allow minor adjustments.

You perhaps notice that the wires (in **4–3**) are not straight, but chinked sharply in some spots. This is for minor adjustments after the wires are in place. If, after your wire is attached, you desire a bit more pull downward, just put a small, sharp bend in the wire with the tip of needle-nose pliers. The wire will not be able to straighten the kink out, and you have effectively shortened it, thereby bringing the branch down a bit more. This wiring technique is acceptable for training, but not for showing, for obvious reasons.

EXTREME BENDING

Large branches may be bent safely by wrapping them first with water-soaked raffia. Then place additional wires longitudinally along the length of the branch and secure them with more raffia. Finally, coil your wire around the branch and bend it slowly. The branch will live even if you hear small cracking sounds. For larger or more stubborn branches, use one of the timed techniques listed at the end of this chapter.

SHAPING WITHOUT WIRE

THE PINCH-AND-GROW TECHNIQUE

The history of bonsai has its roots in China. The Japanese developed the wiring technique only in the last century. Actually, the Chinese province of Lingnan was known for its pinch-and-grow technique several hundred years previously. This method recognizes that certain cuts produce desirable growth and that other cuts will result in undesirable growth.

The success of this method requires you to know and recognize the existing growth patterns on your trees. Here are brief descriptions of those growth patterns and how to prune them (pruning methods A–J, ten in all). You'll find a short list of genera (genus names) affected, so that you'll know how to prune your particular tree.

PRUNING METHOD A

Affected Genera: *Casuarina* (Australian pine), *Pinus* (pine), and *Sciadopitys* (umbrella pine).

The pine family grows by sending out annual new growth called candles. Without damaging adjacent candles, remove dominant candles in their entirety as soon as possible in early spring. The remaining candles are allowed to lengthen until the individual needles are just starting to separate from each other.

If it is large, most of this candle should be gently twisted off. If the candle is medium size, pinch off only half. If the candle is small, allow it to grow. Here is the technique used on a Dwarf Scotch pine, *Pinus sylvestrus* 'Nana' (see **4–4**).

See **step 1** in the drawings on p. 49 (above right). It is too early to prune this pine candle. The emerging needles within the expanding bud are still tan in color and compact. The candle tips are light beige to creamy white. The bud is firm to the touch, with a hairy exterior texture. Wait about ten more days before attempting to prune.

In **step 2**, you'll find a pine ready for pruning. Gently twist and pull the large candle off between thumb and forefinger. It

4–4. PRUNING METHOD A. Candles on this dwarf Scotch pine (*Pinus sylvestrus* 'Nana') may be twisted off.

PRUNING METHOD A (Step 1). It is too early to prune this pine candle, since needles are beige, compact, and have a hairy texture.

PRUNING METHOD A (Step 2). This pine candle is ready for pruning. Twist and pull off the large candle between thumb and forefinger. Pinch and twist off half of the smaller candles.

should separate from the tip of the branch without great effort. Then remove half of each of the remaining two candles. You will need both hands. Grasp the base of the small candle between the thumb and forefinger of your left hand. Then pinch only the outermost tip of the candle with your right hand and gently twist. It will separate from the lower half without damage to the needles.

In late spring and early summer, new candles will appear both at the site where the large candle was removed as well as along the branch farther toward the trunk. Keep the small candles, and allow them to grow to their maximum lengths. Any large candles that appear should be twisted in half, just as you did in early spring. Candles that appear

to be growing in an unwanted direction can, of course, be removed entirely as they appear.

The candles on this pine bonsai (photo **4–5** below) were removed in

4–5. PRUNING METHOD A. Pine bonsai with second crop of candles.

midspring. It is now early summer, and a second crop of candles has appeared. These new candles do not have to be removed, because they are smaller with compact growth.

Notice the horizontal branches and the spacing between them. This allows sunlight to reach into the interior of the tree for better health and insect control. The tree is well ventilated by the wind and, therefore, less susceptible to fungus and disease.

These pine candles (see photo 4–6) are at the right stage of development for easy pruning. With the fingertips, gently twist off the top half of all medium-size candles. Twist off the entire candle if it is

4–6. PRUNING METHOD A. Pine candles ready for pruning.

4–7. PRUNING METHOD A. These are pollen cones, not candles.

unusually large, and keep all petite candles without any pinching back.

The new growth on this pine bonsai (see photo 4–7 on p. 50) is not to be confused with vegetative candles, such as those in photo 4–6 (on p. 50). These tan objects are pollen cones or male cones.

Female cones are the common pinecones we most often see. They are much larger than the male cones and have a coarse, brown, hard structure. These cones are soft, and when touched they release a cloud of spores into the air that can make it difficult for you to breathe. So, caution is advised. They will be short-lived—just a few days—then they will turn soggy and fall off the tree. There is no need to prune them.

bright green new needles trying to unfold. Remove all these buds in their entirety; they are young and tender. If you grasp them between thumb and forefinger and gently pull forward without much force, they will separate.

This early spring pinching will prompt a series of efforts by the tree to grow. New growth will appear

4–8. PRUNING METHOD B. Mountain hemlock (*Tsuga mertensiana*) with buds removed.

PRUNING METHOD B

Affected Genera: *Abies* (fir), *Cedrus* (cedar), *Cephalotaxus*, *Picea* (spruce), *Pseudotsuga*, *Taxus* (yew), and *Tsuga* (hemlock).

In this family of plants, which includes spruce, fir, and hemlock, new early spring growth is protected by a sheath. When this thin covering falls off naturally, you will see an oblong-shape concentration of

everywhere. Pick and choose the buds that you desire, and rub out the buds that you don't want. Observe this technique on the mountain hemlock, *Tsuga mertensiana*, in photo 4–8 (above).

The drawing on p. 52 shows the basic growth pattern for the spruce, fir, hemlock, larch, and similar families. Last year's growth is dark green and contains small buds that appear at random at the base of

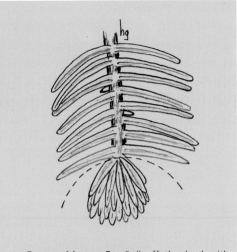

PRUNING METHOD B. Pull off the bud with your fingers. See the dotted line.

needles. They are often difficult to see without a magnifying glass. New growth appears in spring as a rounded collection of chartreuse tender needles. This bud is easily pulled off gently with your fingertips (see dotted line). It should be pulled off in its entirety.

Pruning too late in the year will necessitate the use of fine scissors, because the new stem is beginning to harden into a twig. It is still not too late to prune this way, just more inconvenient.

One month later, the latent buds among the older needles will sprout, thickening and diversifying the branch into secondary or tertiary branchlets. In addition, a replacement bud will develop where the spring bud was removed. It will be smaller than the original and it can be kept.

The new spring buds on the spruce in photo **4–9** (below) are just right for pinching back. Using two hands, grasp the old growth between the thumb and forefinger of one hand, and do the same with the new bud with the other hand. A gentle pull will separate the new and old growth. In a few weeks, new buds will form at the site of injury as well as along the interior of the older branch. Keep wanted

4–9. PRUNING METHOD B. Pinch back the new spring buds on this spruce with thumb and forefinger.

buds and remove growth where it is not needed.

4–10. PRUNING METHOD C. Green-mound juniper (*Juniperus procumbens* 'Nana') requires constant pruning.

PRUNING METHOD C

Affected Genera: Calocedrus, Chamaecyparis (false cypress), *Cryptomeria, Cupressocyparis, Cupressus* (cypress), *Juniperus* (juniper), *Platycladus,* and *Thuja* (arborvitae).

This method is appropriate for most of the needle junipers, cypress, cedar, and arborvitae. New growth appears in midspring, and it is characterized by the gradual appearance of a light chartreuse growth on the outer extension of the branches or at the apex. To stimulate lots of new buds within the branch, allow this growth to continue until it is about 1 inch (2.5 cm) long, then completely remove it.

This pruning technique requires you to prune constantly during the growing season, even up to early autumn. Observe this pruning method on the Japanese green-mound juniper, *Juniperus procumbens* 'Nana' (**4–10**, left).

The juniper family can be quite complex in growth patterns. The drawing (below) is a close-up of a twig of San Jose juniper. It makes a good example because it creates all types of growth found on junipers.

At site A, we see last year's growth hardening into extremely sharp-pointed brown spikes coming from a stem that has turned reddish tan and that is beginning to form bark. This residual growth is what gives many junipers a bad name. The spikes can cause splinters, rashes, and allergic skin reactions. Wear gloves if you are sensitive to them.

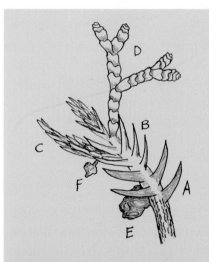

PRUNING METHOD C. San Jose juniper twig demonstrates varieties of growth typically found in junipers. Note growth at sites A–F.

At site B (drawing on p. 53) we see this year's juvenile type of foliage. The spikes are flexible and green. They grow on a green stem. This is the most common type of juniper growth. If you prune growth like that at site B, you'll get growth like that at site C, which is soft, green, and flexible. If you maintain your bonsai properly, you will pull away the tips of C type of growth as they appear. This action will form more soft growth.

Repeated, persistent pruning with your fingertips will produce a soft, green, luxurious branch without hard spikes. With lack of pruning, this soft C-site type of growth will harden into the B-site type of growth, which in turn will become the C-site type of growth in one year.

The D-site type of growth is called needle or ropey foliage. It is prized for bonsai purposes. Unfortunately, in San Jose juniper, it appears only sporadically from untrimmed B growth and at a distance from B growth that makes it impractical for shaping a compact branch. (Upon pruning, it reverts to C-site type of growth.) Fortunately, the Japanese shimpaki or sargent juniper (*Juniperus chinensis* 'Sargentii' or 'Shimpaki') and the blue shimpaki juniper (*Juniperus chinensis* 'Blaauw') grow only the D type of needles. That is why they are so prized as bonsai plants.

The growth at site E is included here because it is often mistaken for a bud or disease. It is a juniper berry—gray, blue, or brown. The developing berry is shown with its stem at site F.

This juniper (**4–11**) is just now beginning to grow in spring. Notice the light green new buds that are forming at the tips of all the foliage from last year. The tip of the tallest branch is exhibiting a different type of growth. This is called juvenile foliage, and it is used to extend a branch where desired.

4–11. Pruning Method C. Juniper with light green new spring buds; tip of tallest branch shows juvenile foliage.

If the branch is already long enough for your design, pinch off strong growth like this as soon as it appears.

Pruning Method D

Affected Genera: *Larix* (larch), *Metasequoia*, *Psuedolarix* (golden larch), and *Sequoia*.

Prune these deciduous conifers only after the branch has grown about 2 inches (5 cm) long. Early spring growth is too succulent to shape or wire.

Rub out unwanted buds as soon as they appear. Allow branch growth to extend several inches (centimeters) before pinching back the tip; the branch will then divide. Secondary growth should be allowed to extend for 2 inches (5 cm) before pruning again; then this branch will divide once more.

4–12. PRUNING METHOD D. Japanese larch (*Larix kaempferi*). Allow secondary growth to extend before pruning again. Remove unwanted buds as they appear.

Give these plants as much sun as they can stand without burning them. Bright sunlight will help compact the new growth. Here is the technique on a Japanese larch, *Larix kaempferi* (**4–12**, above).

PRUNING METHOD E

Affected Genera: *Acer* (maple), *Calliandra*, *Cercidiphyllum*, *Coffea* (coffee), *Cryptocarya*, *Gardenia*, *Lavandula* (lavender), *Luma*, *Melia*, *Osmanthus* (devil-weed), *Oxydendrum*, *Polyscias*, *Punica* (pomegranate), *Rhamnus* (buckthorn), *Ribes* (currant), and *Weigela*.

This pruning is appropriate for any deciduous tree that grows leaves opposite one another along the branch. The new growth in spring will produce a regular, predictable pattern of leaves. Two leaves will first appear as a curled-up clump of foliage that will then open up. The next two leaves will appear shortly after, but rotated 90 degrees along the branch, with respect to the first two leaves.

Select the pair of leaves that are growing horizontal to each other instead of vertical to each other. Prune just in front of them when the branch extends itself farther. Before cutting, make sure that the new growth has extended itself at least two pairs of leaves beyond where you want to cut; this will enhance the "back-budding" (the ability of a tree to expand advantageous buds).

If you prune after only one pair of leaves has emerged beyond the pruning site, new growth will occur only at the branch tip. If you wait until the third or fourth pair of leaves appears, the internodes will be too long. Here is the pruning technique used on a vine maple, *Acer circinatum* (**4–15** on p. 57).

notice that the two opposite paired leaves are oriented along the twig in varying positions. In other words, the first pair of leaves are up and down.

To properly prune this type of tree, locate the pair of leaves that are facing side-to-side on your developing bonsai branch. If you prune where the dotted line indicates, you will force the production of two new sprouts at the base of each leaf, indicated by the arrows.

For best results, be sure there are four or more visible leaves beyond your cut point. If you improperly select a pair of leaves that are oriented up and down, new growth will be unsightly.

4–13. PRUNING METHOD E. Maple bonsai in spring.

The leaves on this maple bonsai (see photo **4–13** above) have come out strong this spring. I plan to exhibit this bonsai in the fall and would prefer to have smaller leaves on it. If I cut off all the leaves, new, smaller foliage will grow in a few weeks.

In early summer the leaves on this maple (photo **4–14** above) were too big. They seem out of scale to the branches and trunk. All the leaves have just been cut off at the

4–14. PRUNING METHOD E. Maple bonsai in summer, with leaves cut off at the stems.

Note the generic drawing (pruning method E on p. 57) of a deciduous tree, such as the maple, that grows opposite leaves. Please

4–15. PRUNING METHOD E. Vine maple (*Acer circinatum*).

stems. In a few weeks, new smaller leaves will sprout, and this bonsai will be ready for a show. While the leaves are off, check for crossing branches, hidden pests, or soft portions of rotting trunk.

Maple bonsai should not be defoliated except when it is an established, healthy bonsai and it is being prepared for showing at an exhibition.

Strong maple shoots such as these (see photo **4–16** below) should be cut back as soon as they appear. The new growth that follows will be smaller and more branched, thus compacting and refining the outline shape of your bonsai.

PRUNING METHOD E. Deciduous tree with opposite paired leaves. Prune at the dotted line to force two new sprouts.

4–16. PRUNING METHOD E. Cut back maple shoots as soon as they appear.

PRUNING METHOD F

Affected Genera: *Agonis, Alnus* (alder), *Andromeda, Annona, Arbutus, Arctostaphylos* (bearberry), *Ardisia, Aucuba, Averrhoa, Azalea, Azara, Berberis* (barberry), *Betula* (birch), *Bougainvillea, Bucida, Buddleia* (Nicodemia), *Bursera, Buxus* (box-wood), *Camellia, Carissa, Carpinus, Castanea, Ceanothus, Celtis, Ceratonia, Cercidium, Cercis, Cercocarpus, Cestrum, Chionanthus, Chrysanthemum, Cinnamomum, Citrus, Cleyera, Comarostaphylis, Corokia, Crataegus* (hawthorn), *Cuphea, Cytisus* (broom), *Daphne, Elaeagnus, Eugenia, Euonymus, Eurya, Fagus* (beech), *Fuchsia, Ginkgo, Guaiacum, Hedera* (ivy), *Hibiscus, Ilex* (holly), *Ixora, Kalmia, Lagerstroemia, Laurus* (laurel), *Leptospermum, Leucothoe, Ligustrum* (privet), *Liquidambar, Lithocarpus, Macadamia, Magnolia, Morus, Myrica, Myrsine, Myrtus* (myrtle), *Nothofagus, Nyssa, Olea* (olive), *Parrotia, Pelargonium, Persea* (avocado), *Physocarpus, Pieris, Platanus* (buttonwood, sycamore), *Populus* (poplar), *Potentilla* (cinque-foil), *Prosopis, Psidium* (guava), *Quercus* (oak), *Raphiolepis, Ribes* (cur-rant), *Rosmarinus, Salix* (willow), *Salvia* (sage), *Sambucus, Serissa, Sophora, Styrax, Syringa, Syzygium, Tilia* (linden), *Trachelospermum, Ulmus* (elm), *Vaccinium, Viburnum* (arrowwood), *Wrightia, Zelkova,* and *Ziziphus.*

These deciduous trees have alternate leaves along the branches. The leaf direction indicates the future direction of the new bud. If you don't want growth upward, don't prune beyond an upward-facing leaf stem. If you desire growth to extend towards the right, prune just beyond a leaf that faces in that direction.

You'll find that leaves will sprout in a very regular fashion: up, down, right, left, up, down, right, left. There will be plenty of opportunities to sculpt your tree properly. Here is the pruning method applied to a Chinese elm, *Ulmus parvifolia* 'Seiju' (**4–17**, opposite on p. 59).

The drawing below is a stylized rendering of a deciduous tree, such as an elm, that grows alternate leaves. New growth will appear at the base of the leaf stem, just in back of any pruning cut.

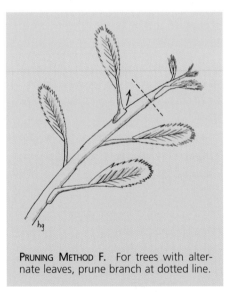

PRUNING METHOD F. For trees with alternate leaves, prune branch at dotted line.

In this drawing we have cut across the stem just beyond a verti-cal leaf. This pruning site is indicat-ed by the dotted line. Cut across the branch at least one-fourth inch (.8 cm) away from the developing leaf bud you want to save. A new branch will form at the base of that leaf and point in the same direction

4–17. Pruning Method F. Chinese elm (*Ulmus parvifolia* 'Seiju'); use this pruning method to sculpt tree. Leaves sprout irregularly.

(indicated by the arrow). If you desire new growth in a different location or direction, simply prune just past a leaf that is pointed in the desired direction. Make sure there are at least two visible leaves beyond the cut point. Pay close attention to the leaf direction. Some trees have only alternate right, left, right, left. Others might display a pattern of right, left, up, down, right, left, up, down. Still other species may be quite random in orientation.

The leaves on this English oak, *Quercus robur* (see photo **4–18**, right), rapidly extend in midspring. The leaves are alternate, just like those in the elm family. Before the leaf internodes get too long, cut between two leaves and get growth like this that's compact and divid-

ing. After pruning, be sure to check the direction of new growth. Remove unwanted shoots (like those shown below) as soon as possible.

4–18. Pruning Method F. English oak (*Quercus robur*); remove unwanted shoots quickly.

PRUNING METHOD G

Affected Genera: *Chaenomeles, Cornus* (dogwood), *Cotoneaster, Forsythia, Malus* (apple and crab apple), *Prunus* (almond, apricot, cherry, nectarine, peach, plum, and prune), *Pyracantha, Pyrus* (pear), *Rhododendron,* and *Rosa* (rose).

This very specialized pruning technique is appropriate to any trees of the rose family, including blackberry, wild rose, cotoneaster, pyracantha, apple, and dogwood, among others. The pruning of this group first year. The next year, prune back the other half, and so on. You can tell by the shape of the new growth which branches were pruned last year, allowing you to avoid pruning away blooms and blooms in progress. See this pruning method applied to the rhododendron 'Impeditum' (**4–19**, below).

Fruiting and flowering trees demand special attention from the grower. We desire these plants for both their foliage and their flowers. The successful pruner can identify the morphological differences

4–19. PRUNING METHOD G. *Rhododendron* 'Impeditum.'

requires that you study the difference between vegetative and fruiting growth. You must maintain some selected vegetative growth, or no fruit will appear.

I recommend heavily pruning half the branches on the tree the between fruiting and flowering buds early in spring. The drawing of this method (p. 61) shows a generalized apple twig just as the leaf buds are beginning to break open. This is an excellent time to prune, because the fruiting spurs are still

Pruning Method G. For rose family trees, prune just as leaf buds begin to break

brown, compact, and brittle.

Compare the shape and location on the twig of the nine leaf buds on the right. They will show a touch of light green at this stage. The four fruiting and flowering spurs on the left are located differently on the stem. They are thicker and protrude at nearly 90 degrees from the branch axis.

Apricot, peach, nectarine, cherry, almond, dogwood, and many others show these differences in early spring. Observe all these morphological differences carefully; then prune with confidence, knowing you are not trimming off flowers before they have a chance to show off.

Pruning Method H

Affected Genera: *Abelia, Aesculus* (horse chestnut), *Albizia, Aralia, Araucaria, Cassia* (senna), *Cedrela, Chamaedorea, Chamaerops* (fan palm), *Cibotium, Cycas, Fraxinus* (ash), *Gymnocladus, Laburnum, Photinia,*

Pistacia (pistachio), *Pittosporum, Podocarpus, Schefflera* (umbrella tree), *Schinus, Sorbus* (mountain ash), *Tamarix* (tamarisk), *Taxodium* (cypress), and *Wisteria.*

These trees produce what look like a number of individual leaves on a branch, but they actually produce only *one* compound leaf. These small "leaves" are really a part of a cluster. Don't make the mistake of thinking you can control growth by pinching or pruning between these "leaves"; nothing will happen.

You must wait until this tree produces another series of "leaves" beyond the first series before you have two real leaves. Then prune off one of these to get the branch to divide. Here is the technique on *Wisteria sinensis* (**4–20** on p. 62).

Plants with compound leaves can be difficult to prune as bonsai. A single leaf can have eleven, thirteen, or fifteen leaflets. These leaflets appear in pairs along the leaf midrib and end with a single leaflet at the tip. A leaf petiole, or attachment, is always bulbous and protects the latent branch bud invisible underneath it.

Pruning Method H. Prune at the dotted line to be sure you remove compound leaves in their entirety.

Notice that the leaflets in the drawing (p. 61) have no such bulbous attachment. If you prune between leaflets, no additional growth is simulated. If you prune where the dotted line indicates, however, a new branch will be formed in the direction of the arrow. This leaf type is found on ash, walnut, pistachio, and wisteria as well as others.

The wisteria in photo **4–20** has compound leaves as well as flowering and vegetative buds. It is a difficult plant to grow as bonsai because efforts to keep the leaves compact will often result in poor flowering.

For best results, allow the bonsai to grow untrimmed in the fall. Then, in the spring, carefully examine each new bud. Save as many flowering buds as possible while heavily pruning back vegetative buds—just as you would an apple tree.

PRUNING METHOD I

Affected Genera and Families:
Adenium, Beaucarnea, Cactaceae (cactus family), *Ficus* (fig), *Manilkara (Achras), Portulacaria,* and *Schefflera* (umbrella tree).

This method is used on tropical trees having milky, latex sap. Growth is constant, since these trees are typically grown in rather sheltered locations such as greenhouses or atriums. Don't use a sharp pruning tool; you will make the plant "bleed" excessively. Use a dull knife, poultry scissors, or a wire cutter.

On large specimens, I prefer to prune with needle-nose pliers because the pruning injury is great, therefore creating a massive load of traumatic acid in the plant. Healing is stimulated by the trauma, and the sap loss stops. An extremely sharp knife will cause a maple to produce gallons of sugary sap, but the blow from the dull

4–20. PRUNING METHOD H. Chinese wisteria (*Wisteria sinensis*) has compound leaves, which can be difficult to prune.

axe will readily heal over. The same principle can be applied to these tropicals. I'm sure you know how long it takes a cut from a razor blade to heal!

PRUNING METHOD I. Use dull scissors to prevent injury to the plant.

Plants that have a milky sap can be poisonous; so take care when pruning them. Wipe off your tools after use. Most pets will exhibit no attraction to the sap, but if your pets are known to chew on house plants, keep them away from freshly pruned tropicals. Cats may be especially vulnerable. Segmented stems, such as those of this jade plant, are best pruned by breaking off unwanted foliage at a convenient joint.

Solid stems, such as those of the *Ficus* (fig tree) genus are best pruned with wire cutters rather than sharp shears. The blunt edges of a wire cutter will slightly damage the stem as it is cut, releasing a trauma hormone in the plant. This sends a signal to the injured area that repair is necessary immediately to stop bleeding. A very sharp cut will make sap ooze for a longer time, thereby weakening the tree.

PRUNING METHOD J

Affected Genera: *Azalea, Bambusa* (bamboo), and *Nandina* (bamboo), and other grasses, lilies, and tubers.

These bonsai are grasses, lilies, or tubers. They are propagated by division. To improve their style, pruning consists of removing distracting growth. When old growth becomes yellow and unproductive, use root trimmers to remove it below ground.

The drawing below shows a young stem of bamboo. Grasses, lilies, bulbs, tubers, and rhizomes can all be dwarfed and used as bonsai or bonsai accompaniment plantings. As new shoots appear, remove the older ones by pruning or by dividing the root masses. Cutting a stem only serves to leave an unsightly scar or a brown tip.

PRUNING METHOD J. Bamboo stem. Remove older shoots as new shoots appear, or divide root masses.

OUTLINE SHAPES

Each genus has its own natural outline shape. Try to learn what trees of a particular genus or species look like in nature before pruning your bonsai. When you trim according to the tree's natural tendencies, you create low-maintenance bonsai. When you fight this natural shape, you have to be constantly pruning, wiring, and pinching in order to achieve the artificial outline.

We recognize some obvious outline shapes in common trees. Pines and maples have a nicely rounded top. Spruces, firs, and hemlocks have a symmetrical, triangular shape with a pointed top. Poplars and arborvitaes have a narrow, rounded, flame-shape body with a somewhat pointed top. Some plants naturally weep or cascade over an edge. Still others hug the ground tenaciously. Many tropical trees rise up to a flat top, and others resemble an inverted broom.

If you are attempting to style an olive tree, for example, find and study an old olive tree in nature. Olive trees in orchards are trimmed for fruit, so be aware of that effect. Use the pinch-and-grow method to achieve an accurate outline shape for a beautiful, low-maintenance bonsai.

4–21. Study trees in nature for the best vision of their future bonsai style. This Austrian pine (*Pinus nigra*) was spotted in, of all places, Austria.

OTHER TECHNIQUES

WEIGHTS

Just like the pull-down method described above and shown in **4–3** (on p. 47 and repeated below), weights many be added to a branch to gradually pull it down.

4–3. Pull-down method of training.

Caution
Gradual bending with a weight is a powerful force. The branch will move a bit every day, so watch carefully and do not overbend it. The pull-down method fixes the branch immediately in its new position. The weight will provide an incessant and constant pull even if the branch bends into the desire place. Remove the weight once in a while to see if it is still needed.

CLAMPS

Commercially produced bonsai clamps or common woodworking clamps can be used to gradually bend a branch. These devices are useful for hard-to-bend, large-diameter branches and trunks. They are also appropriate for brittle species, such as some maples, because the effect is gradual.

See a bonsai clamp in place in photo **4–22**. This trunk is being bent to make it more interesting.

TURNBUCKLES

Similar to the pull-down method is the utilization of turnbuckles. A gradual and persistent force pulling two things together is more powerful than a simple wire, so caution is recommended. Just like the clamp above, a few turns of the screw every week does the trick. Use the turnbuckle whenever you can safely secure your wire without damage. Protection with floral tape is recommended to keep the attachments from cutting into the bark.

4–22. The bonsai clamp used to bend this trunk can also serve as a turnbuckle.

4–23. This fine old branch on a Japanese black pine (*Pinus thunbergiana*) illustrates how to train a pine branch horizontally with a slightly upturned tip.

4–24. A Japanese black pine (*Pinus thunbergiana*) trained in the slanting style. Trees with an extreme slanting style must be wired into their pots or they will tip over in strong winds.

4–25. Before trimming, this European larch (*Larix decidua*) is ragged and unrefined.

4–26. After trimming, the branchlets of this larch are spaced apart and have room for new growth.

4–27. This English oak (*Quercus robur*) is being trained in the broom style.

STYLE NOTES

It is difficult to account for the many differences in style, whether desired or accidental, of various bonsai as well as the differences in the many plant genera, species, and varieties. A combination of training techniques and pruning methods may be desired for individual plants. Just don't overdo it. Train gradually, over time. Of course, the plant's growing region, age, health, and whether it remains evergreen in your area—while it may be deciduous elsewhere—will necessarily affect the outcome.

REPOTTING

5-1. This vine maple (*Acer circinatum*) was repotted as a stump.

REPOTTING BONSAI

This English oak, *Quercus robur* (**5–2**), is ready for repotting. As you can see, the root mass has taken the exact shape of the inside of the container. Last summer, I started noticing that the tree was reluctant to get moist on first watering. I had to return five minutes later and water it again just to get it wet. The tree grew vigorously but had small leaves, a sign that it was beginning to be root-bound. On closer inspection, the trunk would no longer rock back and forth in the container when I tugged on it. When the plant was lifted from the pot, the root ball seemed to contain about seventy percent roots and thirty percent soil.

5–2. English oak (*Quercus robur*) ready for repotting.

5–3. Assemble potting tools.

This is a perfect time to repot this bonsai. Please notice that the new leaves are still absent but that the leaf buds are starting to swell. The danger of freezing is over, and it is time to repot this tree back into its same container. The pot is still big enough.

5–4. Choose the right pot for repotting your bonsai. See chapter one for the many varieties of pots and their suitability for indoor or outdoor use.

First, make sure you have everything you need (5–3). Also helpful at times are a spade, scissors, chopsticks, gloves, and fertilizer.

Carefully separate the compacted roots from the root ball. Try not to tug or yank in a rough fashion. Continue around the top of the root pad between the main visible roots, and be sure not to neglect the muddy area just below the trunk (see 5–5).

Notice the nice beneficial mold that has formed inside the root ball. It has a delicate, heady aroma to it like Camembert rind. That's a sure sign of a healthy root system and soil mix.

Cut off long, trailing roots that you have pulled away from other roots. Use an old hook or one that

5–5. Carefully separate compacted roots from the root ball.

5–6. Cut off long trailing roots with a root hook, dull blade, or scissors.

5–7. Add a fresh layer of bonsai soil to the bottom of a pot washed clean with mild bleach solution.

5–8. Repotting technique using chopstick to pack soil tightly.

does not have to be sharp. The grit in the soil will dull your blades (**5–6**).

Clean your used pot with a mild bleach solution to get rid of potential disease and slimy green scum. Replace the screens in the drain holes if necessary, and add a fresh layer of bonsai soil to the bottom of the pot (see **5–7**).

Place the tree in the container, and check the height of the exposed roots. If they are too low, add more soil to the empty container. If they are too high, you may need to remove more roots from the underside of the root pad. Add a layer of fresh soil to the top and side of the pot.

Using firm strokes with a chopstick, make sure that the bonsai soil is packed tightly into all the air pockets that might be in the loose root mass (see **5–8**). Keep adding soil until no more can be poked inside. You may notice some yellow beads in the soil mix. These are slow-release fertilizer pellets. (Refer to chapter nine for their use.) Water the transplanted bonsai thoroughly right away. Water daily for the next ten days; then go back to your normal watering schedule in which you wait for the soil to become dry between waterings.

The finished tree in photo **5–9** is ready for spring. There is room for new roots to grow. The tree has fresh-draining bonsai soil, slow-release fertilizer for nutrition, and it even got a bit of a haircut. I evened out the outline shape a bit. Compare this tree to that in **5–2**. There is nothing to do now but stand back and watch it grow.

5–9. Finished repotted tree, English oak (*Quercus robur*).

5–10. Vine maple (*Acer circinatum*) ready for its first bonsai pot.

5–11. Here's the root system intact, without any soil.

TRANSPLANTING NURSERY STOCK

This ugly-looking stump is going to make a beautiful bonsai someday. Its trunk is gnarled and half-dead. Its branches are few and poorly placed, but this vine maple, *Acer circinatum,* is ready for its first bonsai pot (see **5–10**).

This time we will not use a root hook at all. We want to see the structure and exact position of each root so that we can begin to style this tree. The only way we can do that is to completely remove all the soil. This is best done with water pressure from a hard blast with the hose—outside, of course.

As you can see in **5–11**, after a blast with the hose, the root system is now completely devoid of all soil.

> **CAUTION**
> Do this procedure only in early spring when the leaf buds are still tight. Once the plant begins to leaf out, it starts to use the roots, and there is danger of damaging the new white root tips. Notice the complete absence of fine white root hairs in this mass. They are all tan in color and dormant. It is safe to cut them anywhere.

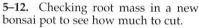

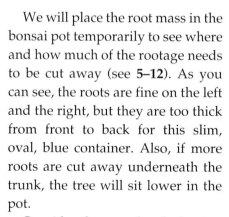

5–12. Checking root mass in a new bonsai pot to see how much to cut.

5–13. Here's the completed planting in a new pot.

We will place the root mass in the bonsai pot temporarily to see where and how much of the rootage needs to be cut away (see **5–12**). As you can see, the roots are fine on the left and the right, but they are too thick from front to back for this slim, oval, blue container. Also, if more roots are cut away underneath the trunk, the tree will sit lower in the pot.

Consider the completed planting in photo **5–13**. The tree appears nestled nicely in this thin container after the excess roots have been cut away. The dead section in the front of the base of the trunk has been scraped clean of all soggy and loose bark. It will be allowed to dry in the sun this summer before I apply lime sulfur to protect the barkless areas. One-third of the way down from the top of the tree is a large knot of dead burl that will be reduced in size a bit next year. I felt that this tree had suffered enough for one year.

Notice that the sprawling long branches have been removed, saving the nicely placed smaller ones. With constant pinching back this spring as the tree leafs out, this bonsai should not need any wiring. It promises to be quite a nice bonsai, in time. Compare this photo (**5–13**) to photo **5–10**. It should be easy to

5–14. Vine maple (*Acer circinatum*). See how the stump we worked with and repotted (**5–10** to **5–13** on pp. 74 and 75) has become a lovely summer tree. It has fulfilled its promise as an appealing bonsai subject.

see the potential I saw in the original old stump. Choosing good nursery stock depends on having a vision for the future bonsai shape.

This is how the tree looks in early summer (**5–14** above). The leaves have come out strong and healthy, perhaps a little too big for now. Simply prune away the biggest leaves, and pinch back strong,

unwanted buds to keep the bonsai in its best form. Eventually—by fall—the leaves will be smaller and more to scale for the trunk and pot.

WOUNDS AND DEADWOOD

Here are a few helpful hints about dealing with dead branches and wounds in bonsai. Natural dead-

5–15. Lodgepole pine (*Pinus contorta* 'Murrayana') with one side broken off.

wood should be kept as clean and dry as possible. Water the roots only, and limit exposure to rain.

Note how the entire left side of this lodgepole pine, *Pinus contorta* 'Murrayana,' (see **5–15**) is dead and has been broken off by natural forces. Observing such natural breaks will teach you how to carve a scar to make the bonsai look natural.

Carve dead branches to look like natural

5–16. This large wound was carved to resemble deadwood.

5–17. We can learn from the natural root spread of an older tree.

driftwood. Cutting them off just leaves an unsightly scar. Carve wounds to look like natural dead-wood (**5–16** on p. 77). Also study the root spread of older trees in the ground, like those in the photo **5–17** (above), to help you achieve a similar result in a bonsai container.

CHAPTER SIX

WATERING

6–1. Traditional copper Japanese bonsai watering can. Note the fine spray that results when the hands are held high. When the can is slightly tilted toward the plant, only a trickle of water falls from the nozzle.

THE TRADITIONAL WATERING CAN

Watering bonsai can be as difficult or as easy as you want it to be. When I was a bonsai apprentice in Japan, I learned how to carefully water priceless trees with a watering can similar to that in photo **6–1**. When I graduated from my apprenticeship, my mentor gave me his watering can—an act of generosity and symbolism. He was acknowledging the fact that I had graduated, and he entrusted me with the life or death of his private collection. Watering or lack of watering does indeed mean the life or death of a plant in a container. Once the tree is in the pot, you are responsible for its care. Nature can no longer do the job.

Most bonsai containers are relatively small compared to containers used in the nursery trade. Nursery growers use deep pots designed to retain moisture longer than bonsai pots can. It is mostly an aesthetic problem. I am sure you can visualize how unfinished a nice bonsai would look planted in a black plastic nursery container. The tree would perhaps be healthier, but its appearance would be inadequate.

Once I returned to the United States after my training in Japan, I set up my first bonsai nursery. Starting small, I was happy and content to use the watering can I had been given. The daily experience of using this vessel was meaningful and profound. It helped me develop an awareness of the plants' moisture needs and provided a link to my upbringing in the Oriental art.

This miniature bonsai *Rhododendron* 'Blue Diamond' (see photo **6–2** below) is only 10 inches (25 cm) high. The container is only the size of the palm of your hand. It requires regular watering, four times a day; in hot days, even more. It is a sixty-five-year-old rhododendron that likes to be moist. This is a very beautiful bonsai, but it's definitely not one we could classify as low maintenance.

6–2. Miniature rhododendron (*Rhododendron* 'Blue Diamond'). Miniature bonsai usually require high maintenance and repeated watering in summer.

THE HOSE-END BONSAI NOZZLE

Before long, I was taking care of over a hundred bonsai. The watering can was inadequate. I was getting tired of the many trips to the faucet necessary to get it filled—especially in summer.

When my collection grew to over two hundred trees, I relented and purchased my first bonsai watering nozzle (**6–3**). Wow! What a relief and convenience. I look back at those years with the watering can with fond memories. However, now I happily pick up the bonsai hose nozzle and go over my trees in minutes rather than hours.

6–4. Keep natural deadwood as clean and dry as possible. Water the roots only, and limit exposure to rain.

Observe the proper way to water using a hose-end nozzle (**6–3** below). Notice that the water pressure is low, and the water rises up out of the end and falls gently on the soil surface.

6–3. The bonsai watering nozzle on this hose reduces the chore of daily watering.

AUTOMATIC WATERING SYSTEMS

As my collection grew still larger and my out-of-town lectures and appearances increased, I had to adjust my watering regime. With 2,000 bonsai to care for and my being gone for a week every month, I came to rely on an automatic sprinkler system for the bulk of the watering chore—always supervised by a friend, neighbor, or employee, I might add. Over the years, I have tried and failed with many systems. The best by far has been the drip watering system.

The drip system is inexpensive, easy to install, and flexible to your custom watering needs. All the plumbing is aboveground for easy inspection and maintenance. Replacement parts are as near as your local hardware store or nursery outlet. The system can be easily changed with the weather, number of plants, individual watering needs, and physical layout of your bonsai area. Even if you have merely a dozen bonsai, this easy-to-install system can save you hours of watering labor and free your time for other activities.

The first drip system I installed worked perfectly the first time I turned it on. It functioned so well, it was scary. Initially, I went to the hardware store, and when I saw all the bins of transformers, filters, emitters, and hoses, I began to feel inadequate to the task. A starter kit gave me the hookups I needed for my outdoor water faucet, complete with hose and water emitters for a few plants. The diagram and instructions for installation and application were so easy, I thought I must be doing something wrong. Everything could be assembled by hand-tightening joints together just as you would fasten a hose to a faucet—no tools, solder, pipe wrenches, or digging. There was even a timer that needed no wiring. It operated on flashlight batteries.

Once your custom-built system is in place, you can go to the beach or mountains and still have a bonsai collection at home. I still highly recommend having a neighbor come over to make sure the system is working the way it should.

A squirrel can dislodge an emitter while burying a nut, the batteries may turn suddenly weak, or you may have forgotten to turn on the water faucet in your haste to depart. These systems are not foolproof, but they come close. They are definitely useful tools for making your bonsai low maintenance.

CHAPTER SEVEN

CARE AND MAINTENANCE

7–1. Chinese elm (*Ulmus parvifolia*) can be grown indoors or outdoors.

THE ZONE SYSTEM

All around the world people are concerned that the plants they buy be appropriate for where they live. Most nurseries do not want dissatisfied customers, and they usually stock plant material that is appropriate for the local climate. After all, they have to take care of the plants successfully before they are sold. Most countries have an agricultural department which oversees the timber industry, food crops, pests, diseases, and the import and export of plants, etc. Most of these organizations have established a zone system for different regions that will help identify which species will survive well in your area.

I follow two such systems, that of the U.S. Department of Agriculture and that of Sunset publications. These systems help to identify, to an accurate degree, whether or not your species is appropriate for your area. Please note that the maximum and minimum temperatures listed for each zone are for plants *in the ground*. Special care must be taken for plants in containers, especially bonsai.

I live in Sunset zone 6. If I select plant material for bonsai purposes, I check on those plants in zone 7, which has a slightly harsher winter climate. If you live in Phoenix, Arizona, you are in Sunset zone 13. Residents of Phoenix who grow bonsai would be well advised to select their bonsai material from zone 12, however, because it has a slightly harsher climate and the plants in containers will have a greater chance of living in Phoenix.

NATIVE PLANTS

In every climate where we might grow bonsai, we find myriad native plants growing and thriving in the ground around us. Look carefully at these local specimens. You might find an unusual yet beautiful flowering shrub or a drought-resistant conifer not mentioned in any bonsai book.

I have seen some incredibly attractive bonsai made with plants that are considered common pest shrubs or trees. Even ground covers can make a nice cascading accompaniment planting. With a permit from your local ranger station or agricultural extension service, most areas will allow digging. Just give them a call. Inexpensive, readily available, and low-maintenance plants may be right in your backyard or nearby natural landscape.

I have enjoyed seeing some of

7–2. Position bonsai benches so that you can readily observe trees from inside the house. This will aid your care and maintence and provide security.

these unusual native plants growing as bonsai over the years. Remember: what is common or mundane in your area is exotic in another. Happy collecting!

WINTER CARE

Use the zone system to select appropriate plants for your local area. Favor using native plants to increase your chance of growing success. In chapter two, we looked at a vast array of potential plants for bonsai that were tired and true. Presuming that you have carefully selected plant material with these factors in mind, then winter care becomes easy. All you have to do is prepare in advance for its arrival.

It is necessary to generalize about various regions of the world in order to complete this chapter. I will begin by eliminating all geographic regions where it never freezes; bonsai growers in those regions have no unusual winter

7–3. Set up a small display table in your home. You can enjoy some of your outdoor bonsai, like this beech, inside for a few days at a time.

problems. They might have summer difficulties, but they can basically ignore the problems. Others have growing problems in more temperate climates.

Another large geographical area is characterized by having some freezing weather in winter. It is not unusual to have to protect sensitive species, especially those listed previously as partially outdoor plants. Simply bring them indoors in winter.

outside in the shade during the summer. As soon as autumn temperatures begin to drop, they become indoor plants. Have a place for them prepared for seasonal changes.

The next wide geographical band contains perhaps the most variety and number of bonsai. This area includes the most bonsai-growing countries: Japan, China, Korea, the United States, southern Canada, the British Isles, northern Europe, and Asia. An equivalent band of tem-

7–4. Make sure your pines and junipers get plenty of ulfiltered sunlight.

The Chinese elm (*Ulmus parvifolia*) is a good example. It can be grown indoors or out (see **7–1** on p. 83). Once it turns its fall color like this, it can become an indoor plant for the winter. In this area, tropical plants or indoor plants are grown

perate weather runs in a circle in the Southern Hemisphere, touching southern South America, South Africa, Australia, and New Zealand. In these areas, the winter care of plants in containers becomes problematic.

Outdoor bonsai need to feel the seasons. This sets their internal clocks to shed old needles, put on new growth, and turn fall colors. They do not, however, need to freeze—they tolerate a freeze, but they do not need it in order to survive.

In those areas where you have only a few deep freezes every year, the best plan is to simply bring the bonsai into a protected area for a few days. They do not need light for even as many as five days. They will be fine in your garage or unheated utility room. As soon as the freezing weather passes, put the bonsai back out on their shelves.

For geographical areas where snow is normal, a cold frame dug into the ground seems to be the favored bonsai treatment. Most gardeners in these northern regions are familiar with the purpose and function of these structures for protecting hardy perennials, bulbs, pota-

7–5. This 300-year-old vine maple (*Acer circinatum*) is just beginning to show its fall color.

7–6. Miniature rhododendron (*Rhododendron*) in full bloom in spring.

7–7. Here is the miniature rhododendron in summer. The blooms have wilted; now is the time to prune.

7–8. After pruning in summer, here is how the miniature rhododendron looks. Observe its outline shape.

7–9. Here is the lovely miniature rhododendron in fall. Enjoy the autumn colors before the leaves fall off.

toes, and the like. Consult your local agricultural extension service for construction plans for cold-frame design. Make sure it is large enough to fit the future bonsai you are going to have when you begin to get addicted.

PESTS

INSECTS

Not all insects are harmful to bonsai. In fact, most insects could not care less about our tiny trees, and we should just leave them alone even if we see them on the foliage. They may be there just to sun themselves or they may be stopping on their way to another destination. There is no need to run for a bottle of some obnoxious poison at the first appearance of a bug.

With insects in particular less control by you means more control by birds, other insects, and other natural biological agents, such as fungi and bacteria. Perhaps the greatest advantage to gardening with bonsai is their size. If we see a potential pest, we can observe it carefully, identify it, and take appropriate action with only tweezers. Think of the orchard farmer, who does not have that option.

Common aphids are easy to identify and eliminate with a strong spray of water or by misting with insecticidal soap. Other pests are tougher and require stronger measures. We are all familiar with hard-scale insects, spittle bugs, cottony scale, and other fixed insects that invade our plants. A cotton swab dipped in spray oil will disturb their protective coating and smother them with oil at the same time, a very effective treatment. Remember, bonsai are small. We can cure their problems simply and easily.

Perhaps the toughest insect pests are the kind that bore into the wood itself or hide inside the foliage. These include termites, beetles, gall aphids, and such. These are best handled by a combination of good prevention and cure. Every winter, clean up debris around your benches that could attract boring insects. They are attracted to rotting mulch, firewood, and dirty bonsai benches.

Make sure that all the deadwood on your bonsai is clean, free of soft spots, and treated every summer with lime sulfur where there is no bark. (See **7–10**.) Just paint the lime sulfur on, full strength, with a small artist's brush.

7–10. Carve dead branches to look like natural driftwood. Paint lime sulfur on exposed, barkless branches each summer.

7–11. This old maple trunk needs to have the rotten portion carved away.

The old maple trunk in **7–11** (above) needs to be carved out. It has soft places in it that are rotting away. Any carving tools will work, from a simple pocketknife to an electric die grinder with router bits. Then, the hollowed-out area will be painted with lime sulfur to protect it from moisture, insects, and disease. The lime sulfur also bleaches the wood so that it becomes a nice driftwood-gray color.

For persistent borers or heavy infestation of damaging insects, a few light applications of a systemic insecticide will take care of the problem. Follow the directions on the manufacturer's label. Mix only enough to treat your trees; you don't want to have to dispose of excess insecticide.

Sowbugs, earwigs, ants, spiders, grasshoppers, and most beetles do no harm to your trees. Physical removal is best. Slugs and caterpillars, however, can ravage a maple tree overnight. They are voracious eaters of tender foliage. If you see slugs around your bonsai, leave a mostly empty can of beer around for them to drink. They will find it. Caterpillars can be removed with tweezers.

See the stylized drawing of an oak leaf (on p. 91). On this leaf we see four different kinds of damage. Sometimes we notice that the leaves on our bonsai appear to have been nibbled upon by an insect, so we automatically reach for the bug spray. Instead, observe closely the type of damage you see. It may not be caused by an insect at all.

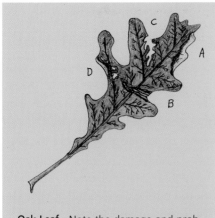

Oak Leaf. Note the damage and probable causes. Sites A–D on the leaf are explained on pp. 91 to 92.

At site A, the outer margin of this leaf appears brittle and light brown, and it has a dark border between it and the healthy green portion of the leaf. Some of the light brown portion may appear torn or missing. This is the classic appearance of sunburn, windburn, or a combination of both. Usually, the affected area of the leaf is pointed toward the southwest (at least in northern latitudes). Move the tree to a more sheltered location.

At site B, the leaf appears broken or torn. Note that the damage has crossed over the midrib of the leaf. Insects will not do this type of damage.

There is very little leaf tissue missing, and the damaged margin is only slightly dried out. The top half of the leaf will probably dry up and fall off because the main nutrient pipeline has been severed. This is purely mechanical damage. An object struck the plant—perhaps a wagging dog's tail, a falling branch, excess wind, or hailstones. You may have even inadvertently cut it while pruning nearby. This is no cause for alarm or treatment. Just cut off the leaf.

At site C, the rounded and scalloped edges of this damage are typical of that done by a caterpillar. Notice how the tender part of the foliage is eaten away and the veins were avoided. The best solution is to find out where the caterpillar is hiding. It's probably curled up in an adjacent leaf taking a nap or finding water near the drain hole of your pot. Simply remove the guy.

7–12. A sure sign that leaf damage is caused by fungus rather than insects: insects do not leave behind a delicate network of untouched leaf veins. They begin at the leaf's edge and avoid the tougher veins.

At site D, this appears at first glance like sun scald on the margin, but holes in the leaf appear nearby. Some of these holes are not all the way through the leaf. Often the condition is more obvious on the underside of the leaves. This is fungus. Treat the plant with a systemic fungicide.

DISEASE

Plant diseases are not like human diseases. Most molds and fungi are a beneficial and important factor in compost formation and soil fertility. But unhealthy or susceptible plants are subject to disease from these agents as well. It is all part of the natural order of living things. They tend to rot and decay and are recycled back into the soil. It's just that we would prefer that our prized bonsai not become compost too quickly.

Prevention is the best cure. Clean up yard debris as soon as possible. Sterilize your bonsai bench annually with a half-strength bleach solution. Isolate any problem trees, like roses and elms. They have a tendency to get black spot and powdery mildew.

The hornbeam leaves in the photo (see 7–13) have sooty mold, white fly, and mildew on them. These diseases and pests are simply overwintering on these dead leaves, waiting to attack the new growth in spring. Throw them away in a leaf bag, mulcher, or compost pile. Do not allow them to remain on or near your bonsai.

Most bonsai diseases are best treated with a systemic fungicide. You'll find many types and brands on the market. Ask your local nursery for one available in your area. Bringing in a sample branch of your problem tree will also aid in identification of the pest as well.

Avoid watering too close to dusk. A tree that is wet all night long on a dry summer night is a target for mold or mildew. I never water after four o'clock in the afternoon, even on the hottest days. Also, if possible, water the soil only, not the foliage. Most outdoor trees do not need the spray on their leaves; it only contributes to disease problems.

7–13. Hornbeam leaves with sooty mold, white fly, and mildew.

MAMMALS AND BIRDS

Of all the common large pests of bonsai, perhaps the trickiest to control is the squirrel. Squirrels seem to want to dig up bonsai soil in order to plant their nuts and seeds. If you feed nearby squirrels, you will no doubt have problems with this. If you want to get rid of them, there are nice live traps you can set out for relocating the pest(s) a few miles away. A light sprinkling of cayenne pepper around your pots will discourage them from bothering your trees.

Rats and mice are found in both urban and rural areas. Various baits and traps are available to get rid of them. They will eat the soft new cambium on your bonsai.

Larger mammals, such as raccoons, nutrias, beavers, and opossums, can be live-trapped and removed. They will all eat bonsai and make quite a mess—just overnight. Often, you can get an animal control agency in your area to help. The agency has the knowledge and equipment to do the job.

Deer can be a problem in forested locations. They like to eat delicate leaves and flowers. The best solution seems to be to fence your bonsai area. Make sure it is fenced well and that the fence is up to eight feet tall. A light sprinkling of blood meal and bonemeal seems to help keep deer away, although it might attract neighborhood cats.

Birds can be a problem, but they seem to be attracted to nuts and seeds in the area. If you maintain a birdfeeder, avoid the use of peanuts, filberts, pecans, and other larger nuts that attract aggressive blue jays. The jays will stick around to look for more nuts and insects among your seedling and cutting beds, and they will tear off the moss that you so carefully nurtured in bonsai pots.

FERTILIZERS

Since we are concerned with low-maintenance bonsai, let's consider low-maintenance fertilizers. There are three ways to go. Choose the method that appeals to you and that's available and convenient.

SLOW-RELEASE FERTILIZERS

Slow-release fertilizers are large solid granules of fertilizer that are sprinkled on the surface of the soil. Each time it rains or you water your bonsai, a bit of nutrient dissolves from the granules on top and runs down into the pot. Use a well-balanced fertilizer with a fairly low nitrogen rating. The nitrogen–phosphorus–potassium (N–P–K) analysis is found on all fertilizers. You are looking for numbers such as 5–10–10, 3–7–8, or 10–15–10. Avoid high-nitrogen products like 18–6–12, 15–3–6, or 21–8–5. The first number indicates the nitrogen content, and it should be at or below the other two numbers that indicate the amount of phosphorus and potassium for bonsai.

Fertilizer Spikes

Fertilizer spikes are slow-release pellets that you push into the soil and that slowly dissolve. For best results, choose plant spikes for blooming plants.

Liquid Concentrated Fertilizer

These are usually green or blue liquids designed for use with a watering can. Simply dissolve a few drops of the concentrate in your watering can, and apply as you water your trees. A half-strength application once a week should be sufficient for most bonsai. If the label instructions say "10 drops per gallon," use just five; then apply weekly during the growing season. Never fertilize a dormant plant, a sick plant, or a dry plant. Water first; then apply the diluted concentrate.

7–14. Japanese maple (*Acer palmatum*) Plenty of sunshine and frosty nights will bring out the fall color of deciduous trees. Do not overwater at this time, and stop fertilizing with nitrogen.

INDEX